MW00587382

Learning Science

for Instructional Designers

From Cognition to Application

Clark N. Quinn

ATD Press is an internationally renowned source of insightful and practical information on talent development, training, and professional development.

ATD Press
1640 King Street
Alexandria, VA 22314 USA

Ordering information: Books published by ATD Press can be purchased by visiting ATD's website at td.org/books or by calling 800.628.2783 or 703.683.8100.

Library of Congress Control Number: 2021930866

ISBN-10: 1-952157-45-5
ISBN-13: 978-1-952157-45-5
e-ISBN: 978-1-952157-46-2

ATD Press Editorial Staff
Director: Sarah Halgas
Manager: Melissa Jones
Content Manager, Science of Learning: Alexandria Clapp
Developmental Editor: Jack Harlow
Production Editor: Hannah Sternberg
Text Design: Shirley E.M. Raybuck and Stephanie Shaw
Cover Design: Rose Richey

Printed by BR Printers, San Jose, CA

To all the researchers who advance our understanding of learning, and the designers who apply that research to create effective and engaging learning experiences.

Contents

Preface

If we're truly being professionals about designing learning, there's a clear onus to be aware of what learning science tells us. And that runs from the cognitive story at the core through to the learning prescriptions that emerge. Quite simply, we have a responsibility.

If a doctor pursues approaches unjustified by science, they're liable for malpractice. Similarly, we should be implementing scrutable practices. There are consequences for not doing so. If we use approaches that aren't justified, we can squander resources, but more importantly, we can undermine our own goals. In the worst case, lives are lost. In fact, you'll see that industries with significant potential downsides of getting it wrong practice in ways not typically seen in corporate America. Look at the military and airlines as two examples.

So, we have a responsibility to our learners, our organizations, and ourselves to understand and apply what's known, whether from a deep-seated curiosity and caring, or just because it's what's required of us.

I come from the former category. I was kind of at loose ends, degree-wise. I was tutoring (physics, calculus, chemistry) on campus for some extra income, and taking some computer science courses. I ended up doing computer support for the office that coordinated the tutoring. And a light went on: computers supporting learning! My university didn't have an appropriate degree program (back then, many didn't; I was carrying around decks of punch cards in order to run the computer programs), but it *did* have a way to design your own. So, that's what I did, and learning design and technology has been my career ever since.

I've programmed educational computer games; gone back for a PhD in what was, effectively, applied cognitive science; and gone the academic route: a post-doctoral and then a faculty position. For complicated reasons, I also joined some government-sponsored initiatives in online learning before joining a startup in educational technology. When that went four paws to the moon in the economic chaos that characterized the collapse of the internet bubble, I ended up as a consultant (which went from being a euphemism for unemployed to a way of life).

However, my career has always been about exploring ways to use technology that allow us to pursue our goals more effectively and efficiently.

Along the way, I've maintained a passionate interest at the intersection of four related fields. I've looked at learning—behavioral, cognitive, post-cognitive, social, educational, even *machine* learning—to see what's known. Similarly, I've followed what's known about engagement, including motivation, anxiety, curiosity, drama, and humor, to understand how we create experiences that are meaningful, even transformative. I've also followed technology trends from before personal computers, including artificial intelligence, mobile, content systems, constructed realities (augmented and virtual), and more, to find out what new capabilities we might use. Finally, I've looked at design, including interaction, industrial, graphic, software engineering, and of course instructional approaches, to ensure that we're applying this knowledge in the most useful ways.

That's my mission: Discover how to create experiences that tap into our hearts and apply our minds to achieve useful ends. It's all about strategic learning experience design (LXD). (And through technology, since I'm admittedly a sucker for the latest toy.) Which means I have looked at practical ways to integrate this suite of knowledge. Here, I'm focusing on learning, and its application to instruction.

And, as you'll see, our brains consolidate information. We don't remember many exact details; instead, we remember a synthesis. And that's what I'm doing here. This is not a detailed academic treatise, but rather an attempt to digest and communicate a practical interpretation of what's known about cognition and learning to provide a basis for better design.

I hope you find it comprehensible and useful.

Acknowledgments

There are so many people I owe gratitude to, and I've tried to catalog them in previous books. A few who continue to support me include the following.

Jim "Sky" Schuyler has been a mentor, colleague, and friend since out of college and continuing on. A great role model.

Marcia Conner has been a mentor at stages in my career, providing opportunities and helping me learn important lessons.

My Internet Time Alliance colleagues, instigated by the late, great Jay Cross—Jane Hart, Harold Jarche, and Charles Jennings—all have served to improve my understanding of learning and life.

My IBSTPI colleagues, including Mark Lee, Kathy Jackson, Davida Sharpe, Fernando Senior, Saul Carliner, Florence Martin, and Stella Porto, have been sources of inspiration and learning.

Thanks also to all my colleagues in many different forums; in particular (and in no particular order), Will Thalheimer, Karl Kapp, Patti Shank, Julie Dirksen, Mirjam Neelen, Donald Clark, Jane Bozarth, Jen Murphy, Chad Udell, Connie Malamed, Matthew Richter, Guy Wallace, and the other mythbusters and science interpreters have all helped shape my rigor and understanding. Apologies if I haven't mentioned you! And I'm grateful to so many more colleagues who inspire me and support us all in doing better.

I'm grateful to all the organizations that have given me platforms to share my thinking on how to improve the field, through workshops, keynotes, talks, articles, books, and courses. Thanks to societies, publishers, private organizations, individuals, and more.

Also, thanks to the organizations that have brought me in to work with them. It's a deep pleasure to be able to get hands-on with real problems and try to "Quinnovate" some new ideas. I've learned so much from these opportunities with public and private companies, not-for-profits, governmental bodies, educational institutions, and more.

I'm also grateful to Justin Brusino, Alexandria Clapp, Jack Harlow, Melissa Jones, Caroline Coppel, Hannah Sternberg, Shirley Raybuck, Rose Richey,

Stephanie Shaw, and the rest of the ATD team who've pushed and supported me through this experience. This book exists because of Justin and Alexandria is immeasurably better because of Alexandria, Jack, Hannah, and Caroline, and looks great thanks to Melissa, Shirley, Rose, and Stephanie.

My family—Erin (who served as a reviewer of an early draft), Declan, and most of all, LeAnn—have been stalwart supporters. With love and gratitude.

CHAPTER 1

Introduction to Learning Science

- What is learning science?
- Why we need learning science
- How learning science is conducted
- How to find learning science resources

---

plunger (plŭn′jər)
The plunger in the pump was broken. A *plunger* is a:
    (a) dolphin
    (b) pump part
    (c) brown car
—A found example of online learning

What possible learning purpose does this example serve? The question comes right after the content. It asks a question where the answer is implied by the immediately preceding material, and the alternatives are nonsensical or silly.

This example is emblematic of why we need learning science. Because when we design learning experiences, we want to achieve an outcome. And, if we don't do it according to learning science, we could waste our stakeholders' resources and our learners' time.

To address the need in this book, we'll go through basic cognitive architecture, and then the learning phenomena (cognitive artifacts like mental models) of reasoning that arise from this architecture. We'll look beyond cognitive to emotional aspects, and we'll point out the implications for learning experiences and the design of specific elements.

First, however, we should establish more about the science we're investigating.

What *Is* This Learning Science?

Learning science is, not surprisingly, the scientific study of learning. It means looking at how learning works, and also what facilitates and hinders learning. It provides a strong basis for designing instruction. It is relatively new, however.

Our brains are the core organs of learning. We perceive the world, act, observe the outcomes, and reflect. Consequently, studying learning comes from studying the mind. The ancient Greeks philosophized about how our brains work, but scientific exploration of learning really only began with Hermann Ebbinghaus's studies of memory in the 1800s (Figure 1-1).

Figure 1-1. Ebbinghaus's Memory Study

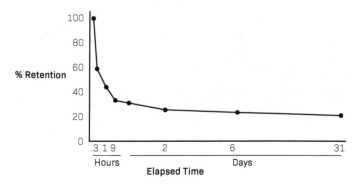

The field of psychology has subsequently gone through several movements, including behaviorist, cognitive, and constructivist. Each of these added insights have furthered our understanding.

The behaviorist school started out by saying that we can't talk about what's going on inside the brain; we only can connect inputs with outputs. This was the era of Pavlovian conditioning and stimulus-response approaches. Robust findings include the value of different reinforcement schedules (think gambling; Figure 1-2) and the Yerkes-Dodson performance-arousal curve.

The cognitive revolution said that we can hypothesize what brain structures must exist. Research showed various facets of our information processing that have stood the test of time. There was a vision that we were formal, logical reasoners.

Revelations that we're not the formal-thinking beings we thought prompted the move to a more *situated*, or constructivist, view of cognition. Here, we realize that our thoughts are an interaction between context and previous experience. We may use concepts differently depending on context, and certain types of reasoning are problematic.

Figure 1-2. Reinforcement Schedules

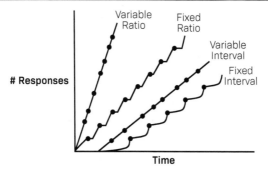

Importantly, psychology isn't the only field that talks about how our minds work. Insight still comes from fields such as philosophy, neuroscience, linguistics, anthropology, and sociology. The field of cognitive science was created to be an umbrella under which these differing elements could be integrated. And it's provided a solid foundation for developments including communication and collaboration practices, interface design, and artificial intelligence.

Learning science is similarly interdisciplinary. Research insights have come from psychological investigations, educational studies, ethnographic approaches, and sociological work. (A side effect is that results from one discipline may not take into account results from another, related discipline.) A growing awareness of this relatedness led to the establishment of the discipline in the 1990s.

Learning science is also global. I was a graduate student in the United States during the establishment of the discipline, and then a post-doctoral fellow. There is so much research done in the US, it was easy for me be focused nationally instead of internationally.

Later, I had the good fortune to take a faculty position in Australia, and quickly (and shamefacedly) learned my awareness of research was blinkered. I was also able to visit global conferences and get exposed not only to the field's interdisciplinary nature, but also to its global cohort of researchers. And it's important to realize, and recognize, that the results and implications properly span cultures and nationalities.

Why Should *We* Care?

Another plausible question is *why* learning science? Why should we understand the underlying cognitive mechanisms, the artifacts and limitations of our mental architecture, and the associated elements? Can't we just follow the resulting precepts of instructional design? I'll suggest that the answer is a resounding "no."

My short answer is that it's a professional imperative. Instructional design is applied learning science. How can we claim to be scrutable in our approaches if we don't track the underlying research, and can't articulate how our designs reflect what is known? Just as you expect your doctor and financial adviser to be applying the latest outcomes, so too should you feel such an obligation when designing learning experiences. We don't want to be guilty of design malpractice, after all.

The longer answer starts with the realization that instructional design is a dynamic field. Even David Merrill, one of the founders of and forces in instructional design (and a truly nice person to boot), has had phases of change. His Component Display Theory, for instance, progressed to ID2, and now he's on about a "pebble in a pond." New understandings in learning science drive the need to revise our approaches.

The foundations we build our design processes on have shifted. Instructional design emerged as an artifact of World War II, when behaviorism was in force. As we've gone through the cognitive era and into a post-cognitive constructivist awareness, our design bases similarly adapted. Each of those transitions has had implications for what we think learning is, and consequently what makes sense as pedagogy.

Recent understandings continue to drive our approaches. To be able to react to new approaches means grasping some fundamental underpinnings. Separating them from other explanations is a critical component of being a successful practitioner. (I once was presented with a "hydraulic" model of learning, an engineering metaphor misapplied to understanding our thinking!)

This implies a second reason to understand the basics: Folks will continue to propose new approaches. They will come to these approaches sometimes from pure conviction, rightly or wrongly, but also for commercial reasons. Practitioners need to be careful about evaluating new claims. With an understanding of the basic mechanisms, you're better prepared to avoid the learning myths that plague our field (as I documented in my last tome, *Millennials, Goldfish & Other Training Misconceptions*).

Also, instructional design has great recommendations, such as we see in the movement to evidence-based methods as discussed in recent books by Ruth Clark and by Mirjam Neelen and Paul Kirschner. Thus, a third reason is that there are still gaps that prescriptions won't fill. Making good choices in lieu of guidance depends on understanding the mechanisms as suggested by theories.

How Does One "Learning Science"?

Learning science is the result of the usual processes of science. While there are many different methods, the basis we should be using is the result of experimentally tested and statistically validated approaches.

A major distinction is between quantitative and qualitative studies. In quantitative studies, you have clear metrics that are objectively obtained, such as scores on tests or observationally clear performance while completing tasks. Here we typically have some subjects working in one way (such as under the experimental treatment), and a control group in another, typically pre-existing, way, and we then look at the outcomes.

Statistics are used to determine with some degree of certainty whether the outcome is due to chance (Figure 1-3). It is a probabilistic game, because even significant tests have a chance of being false 5 percent of the time. This is one of the reasons it is preferable if the results are replicated. Reputable reports, such as those in a peer-reviewed journal or book chapter, will detail the study sufficiently so that someone can conduct the same study. And this happens.

Figure 1-3. Statistical Significance

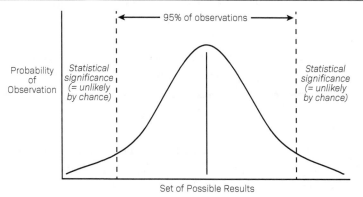

Note that despite their empirical nature, experiments tend to be driven by theory. While there are some purely experimental studies ("What will we find?"), most times someone creates a hypothesis, and then tests it. For instance, someone may say, "Hmm, one prediction of cognitive load theory might be that we need to integrate labels into diagrams to keep people from generating more mental overhead by looking back and forth between them, trying to integrate the element and its meaning." They run a test, and find out if it's true (spoiler: it is).

Qualitative studies similarly use the scientific method, but they take data that's more complex than just numbers (verbal protocols, interviews) and code it, and then look for patterns. Typically, you need some controls on the interpretation to support the resulting analysis, such as someone independently coding a subset of the data and looking for the agreement. For my PhD thesis, for instance, I coded transcripts of subjects' verbal efforts in problem solving. As a control, I also hired a student to code a subset of the data using my rubric, and checked to see that the coding was reliably consistent. Finding (and reporting) that the degree of agreement was sufficiently high meant that we could then report that the data was reliably coded.

Importantly, your data should get reported in a journal. What this means is that you write it up in unambiguous language and peers review it, and it must pass scrutiny. Along with the results, you situate your work in others', via a literature review, and you make clear what the unique contribution is. The peer scrutiny can be a problem, particularly if the work is upending established protocol. There's a whole field of science *about* science, and concepts like Thomas Kuhn's paradigm shift are used to characterize the bigger changes. Yet overall the process works.

Be aware that the language used for journals is an obscure dialect known as academese. This is typically based on English, but uses an esoteric and almost deliberately impenetrable vocabulary. It takes training to be able to comprehend it. Learning to read academese is a valuable skill, but probably not for most folks.

At its core, however, the systematic process of experimentation and theory advancement, as well as theory revision and replacement, is all part of science. And its results are the best basis upon which to determine our approaches.

On the Lookout for Learning Science

As suggested, the best way to track science is to read journals. And, again, not everyone should be expected to read them. The nuances of appropriate methodologies are subtle, and not necessarily of use to all. What to do instead?

Fortunately, there is a cohort of folks who are reliable translators. In addition to the scientists—those who can reliably communicate to laypeople, and that's not all of them—are folks steeped in the traditions (typically with PhDs from experimental programs) but who work in the real world. A number of them continue to serve as valuable proponents for applications of the science.

These translators write blog posts, articles, chapters, and books. They present via webinars, conferences, and keynotes. You should know them, listen to them, and, of course, hire them. They can do workshops to educate your team, consult to improve your processes, and help you plan to better align. They're the source of the best principles to apply to your practices. I maintain a list of the best translators at quinnovation.com/translators.html. And you should know the places where translation writings aggregate. Not every place is rigorous about the quality of its materials.

The Rest of the Book

With that all said, what am I going to cover? I think it's important to work our way up from the fundamentals of the brain to what that means for learning. This means a steady progression through several areas (Figure 1-4).

Figure 1-4. Book Structure

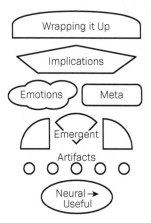

First, we'll look at our cognitive architecture using a "stores and processes" model. Here we'll learn the basic information-processing cycle, from sensed signals to long-term memory.

The artifacts for learning that emerge from this architecture are next. Tied in to attention and working memory limitations is cognitive load. Similarly, specific elements around models have implications from refining retrieval to developing content.

We'll then review the phenomena that are outcomes of this architecture. We'll look at some more recent frameworks that document some characteristics of our thinking that are not logical, and what that means. This includes looking at processing media.

From there we'll go beyond the cognitive to the emotional—or, rather, affective and conative (who we are and our intent to learn). We'll explore what's known about experience, motivation, and more.

We'll also examine learning to learn. This important area is often neglected, yet it can have an impact on success. This includes a culture of learning.

Then we'll delve into the implications of all this science on the elements of learning design. We'll explore introductions and closings, concept models, examples, and, of course, practice.

And we'll look at the elements in another way, as sets of prescriptions for design. This includes two frameworks and a detailed example.

Overall, our journey is:

+ Chapter 2: Our brains, from the neural level to the level of language
+ Chapter 3: Learning artifacts that arise from our architecture
+ Chapter 4: Some new perspectives with implications for learning
+ Chapter 5: The emotional side of learning
+ Chapter 6: Learning to learn
+ Chapter 7: Learning experience design implications
+ Chapter 8: How it all fits together

That's it—buckle up; it's going to be a wild ride!

Activities

How do you get the most out of this book?

+ Reframe the content, whether mentally, into different terms, or physically, in terms of rewriting core ideas, mind-mapping the content, or sketch-noting it.

+ Reflect on how the content explains things you've experienced in the past, including good and bad learning.
+ As you work through the content, ask: What does this imply that I should do (differently)?
+ Make it a habit to track learning science translations and translators.

CHAPTER 2

From Neural to Useful

- The information-processing cycle
- Stores: sensory, working, and long-term
- Processes: perception, attention, rehearsal, elaboration, and retrieval

Some years ago, there was a spate of "brain training" apps released that were supposed to exercise your thinking skills. And, you'll notice, they've largely disappeared. That's because training on some things doesn't transfer to other, dissimilar things.

We are quick to latch on to ideas that seem good. The important thing is to drop them when they prove to be ill-advised. Yet, in learning and development, certain ones continue to be marketing draws despite their lack of efficacy.

There's been a current surge of approaches labeled "neurolearning" and "brain-based" learning (the latter of which is only slightly more helpful than "leg-based walking," as a colleague suggests), occasionally accompanied by MRI images. New neurological results *are* coming out of the evolving capabilities of imaging, but the suggestion that they have implications for learning and instruction are, well, premature at best. On the other hand, we do have good scientific bases for what we should do.

Cognitive science has established some solid foundations and some new revelations. We can use them as a basis for important prescriptions, and then we can explore elements that add nuances. We need, however, to develop a solid foundation for understanding.

The most useful framework is to think about information passing from knowledge store to knowledge store via cognitive processes. All this is inferred on the basis of experiments, but it explains the data better than competing frameworks. Underpinning it all *is* a neural layer, but that's not the best basis for the purposes of learning design.

From Neural to Useful

Our brains are massive networks of interconnected neurons. When we think, we activate parts of this network as patterns. And, when we learn, we essentially strengthen the connections between neurons. As the saying goes: "The neurons that fire together, wire together." This makes the process of learning neural at its core. However, certain features of our cognitive architecture mean this is the wrong level of analysis.

It's similar to the way an individual pixel on a screen isn't the whole picture (Figure 2-1). Examining, or activating, one pixel won't create the scene. It's the relative activation of one with another across the whole screen that makes a picture. Similarly, the excitation of neurons in patterns *is* the thought. A different set of patterns represents different concepts, and shared elements are activated together. Again, we strengthen relationships by triggering the patterns together. And we don't address individual pixels; we provide input that gets processed on top of our existing knowledge to advance our understanding. You and I may store our representation of the word *house* differently, but the word itself will trigger each of our representations.

Figure 2-1. Neural and Pixel Activations

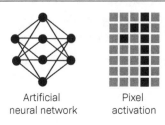

Artificial
neural network

Pixel
activation

There is some simplification in here, but the goal is to give you enough background to comprehend the decisions we'll make about the importance of contexts, the role emotions play, and the gaps that require design process support. There are reasons to do things the way we'll derive, and the more you understand *why*, the better you'll be able to adapt the recommendations to your own circumstances.

Note that accessing individual neurons is an incredibly invasive process. To address an entire concept, you'd have to have access to most of the neurons, with the ability to selectively activate them. At the neural level, that'd mean massive numbers of extremely fine wires connecting to each neuron. That, to me, would mean way too much messing about, with surgery in and around my existing connections. The risk of causing damage is high, and we don't need to do it. There's a far more effective way to activate neurons. Further, we don't strengthen individual neurons alone. There's no leadership neuron, for instance. Again, our thinking is represented by patterns of activity across mass numbers of neurons.

So, we activate these patterns through language and images. Concepts like leadership are represented by certain patterns of activation across our brains. Thus, while our brains are neural, we don't design learning at this level. We typically work by activating concepts in contexts, and explicitly tying labeled things in the world together. This isn't the neural level; it's the cognitive level. It's like how your car runs gas or electricity, but you don't control those directly; you instead control the accelerator pedal and the brake.

In the end, you'll continue to see a lot of "neural" branding in our field. And, sad to say, it's largely hype. As I hopefully just made clear, neural is the wrong level. It's trendy to ride the flash that accompanies the label, but it's misleading. Yes, you're strengthening neural-pattern connections, *but* you're doing so at the cognitive level.

A Matter of Semantics

What happens at the next higher level? Here's where things get real. A theory developed in conjunction with empirical research suggests a picture of stores and processes. That is, information is represented in a series of stores, with processes transferring information between them. The store that learning is ultimately concerned with is the long-term memory. This is where what we've learned is retained for use in action. The interaction between what comes into our conscious awareness and what's triggered by our memory determines the actions we take. This is a simplification, but, again, a useful one. Thus, our goal is to develop our memory (Figure 2-2).

Figure 2-2. Human Cognition Stores and Processes Model

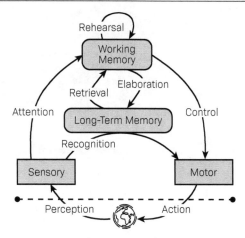

Come to Your Senses

Let's start with the senses. Your senses are your connection to the outside world. Any prompt will be perceived through the senses, so it's the start of the journey. We've regularly been told of the core five, though science now suggests more, including movement, balance, and temperature. And, for some learning, these senses can matter. In most cases, however, we're dealing with sight and sound.

Our processing capacity for the senses differs according to their utility. The "sensory homunculus" is a rendering of the amount of cortex capacity allocated to the different senses (Figure 2-3). What's seen is that the hands, eyes, lips, and mouth capture much of the capacity.

Figure 2-3. Sensory Homunculus (Adapted From OpenStax College)

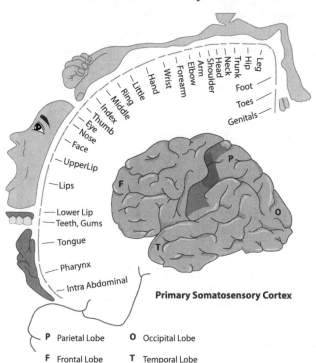

We perceive changes in the world through our senses. Of course, some changes may not be detectable, being outside our range of perception. What we do perceive is captured in sensory store in the form in which it's perceived—so your visual store retains retinal images, your auditory store retains sound changes, and so on. This then makes our perceptions available for processing (Figure 2-4).

Figure 2-4. Perception and Sensory Store

As the previous diagram suggests, sensory inputs eventually result in motor outputs, and then the world responds. (Of course, it's chugging along in the background as we think and act, but our actions can be on the order of milliseconds. Thoughtful actions, of course, take a bit longer, typically at least a second or so.)

> **Learning:** Ensure that any information you want learners to perceive is detectable. Using appropriate channels for information and providing sufficient duration is important. For instance, give learners control over dynamic media so they can pause or restart it; otherwise, information could be lost.

Sight

Sight has been allocated the largest amount of brain processing, which isn't surprising. When you consider the amount of input the retina is providing, you'll recognize the bandwidth required. In fact, we still struggle to fully engage visually with tools like virtual reality (VR) headsets.

Our eyes are designed with a high-resolution color center, and a black-and-white periphery. That periphery, however, is *highly* motion sensitive. Evolutionarily, that makes sense. Motion in the periphery could be dangerous, such as a predator. However, this has downsides. If you remember back to the early 2000s, and webpages with animated gifs on the periphery, you may recall how hard they made it to pay attention to the content in the center. We're wired to orient to the motion. Fortunately, we've mostly eliminated those.

Of course, we're processing only a portion of the energy spectrum. With support, we can expand and detect infrared outside one end of our visual spectrum, and ultraviolet outside the other. Within the spectrum, of course, brightness, saturation, and contrast can matter.

Recognize that not everyone's optical system is optimal, and not everyone is sighted. Color blindness affects close to 10 percent of the population (particularly males). Interestingly, there is more than one kind. In short, it's knocking out one or another of the ways we process color.

Sound

Sound is a very different system. For one thing, sound isn't perceived all at once; it's based on air movement over time at different frequencies. Thus, unlike sight, where there's a possibility for instant recognition, it takes time for the audio-frequency variations to be processed. Volume is another factor.

Similar to sight, sound-processing ability can be interfered with as well. Some folks have trouble with quiet noises, others have problems with particular frequencies, and some have no sound capability at all. (All those loud concerts in my misspent youth have damaged some of mine.) Being sensitive to these differences can include using text alternatives to spoken audio, for instance.

Speech is arguably the highest-bandwidth medium we have. Language has evolved to compact meaning into small textual elements, and it doesn't take much audio to communicate complex concepts. Some argue that the reason we achieved supremacy as a species is the ability to use language.

The semantics of audio go beyond speech. Noises can cue us in if things are going well or not. There's a story that in the days of vacuum-tube computers, you could hear whether your calculation was going correctly or not. Certainly, sounds can indicate whether our cars are running properly, for example, and audio alerts are signals of status changes.

Smell and Taste

Smell and taste can be important, but tend to be both more idiosyncratic *and* difficult to address. They're also linked. Certainly, taste requires some indelicate invasiveness. It is true that some smells can trigger memories. Using smell can certainly help create contexts, when done right. However, doing this reliably is typically an expensive option.

And, again, certain folks are limited in taste or smell. Regardless, these senses are unlikely to be reliable conduits, with one exception. If the learning objective has to do with smell or taste, such as learning to recognize leaking gas or developing a palate as part of becoming a sommelier, of course taste and smell can matter. In general, however, it's a difficult and likely unnecessary addition to most learning programs.

Touch and More

Touch has been touted as the fifth sense, and certainly our entire skin surface is a sense organ. Our hands, in particular, command a considerable proportion of sensory neurons as well. The picture has become more complex, however.

For one, just for the skin, there are three separate areas: touch (any type of contact), temperature, and pressure. That is, we can tell if we've been touched or not, and we can also distinguish between different levels of pressure, and differences in temperature. These can play a role in how one acts, say, with controlling equipment.

Further, scientists have recognized that body feedback is also perceived, and differently than touch in general. For instance, balance comes from the cochlear cells in the ear. Similarly, we can, with eyes closed, move our bodies in particular directions ("Close your eyes and touch your nose") without other feedback. We can *feel* how our body parts are positioned relative to others.

Our motions are how we act on the world, whereas the senses are how the world acts on us. The feedback from a steering wheel, for instance: The "feel" is both a mechanism for us to act on the world and for the world to provide sensory feedback back to us.

Certainly, vibration can provide clues, as we're seeing as we start moving to mobile (the topic of a previous book, *Designing mLearning*) and wearables. And, certain experiences can include motion. I think of rides like Star Tours at Disneyland, where you're in a small, stationary room. However, the room can move a little bit on top of activators. Coupled with a visual experience suggesting flight, the experience can be compelling to the point of disorienting (my spouse won't go).

Sensory Gaps

There are processes to adapt to deficits in vision, audition, and more. For accessibility reasons, we should be mindful. Using different colors that can also be distinguished via other clues provides a mechanism to maintain codings that can still be perceived by the colorblind, for instance. Providing other, redundant, clues can also help. And there are readers that translate text to speech. Consider also having written transcripts for all spoken dialogue.

> **Learning:** Consider accessibility. There are potential limitations in your audience. First, design so that there are redundancies, such as augmenting color with pattern. Second, provide alternatives, such as text of any audio. Third, provide support for alternative mechanisms, such as screen readers.

Like touch and taste, if your learning objectives include motion and physical reaction, they'll need to be part of your ultimate experience design. Given that these factors may be expensive, you may want or need to scaffold into them. Flight training is an example here: It's about maneuvering a plane, potentially under negative conditions, so simulations start simple and gradually get more realistic.

From here, our sense data goes into sensory store.

Everything's Available at the Sensory Store

Our eyes and ears process input into a "sensory store." (So, too, do our other senses.) There are unique ones for each sense, but here we're going to largely focus on vision and, to a lesser degree, auditory signals.

The existence of a sensory store is determined by experimentation, but it has been demonstrated to have particular features. It has capacity equal to our perception; that is, you pretty much capture everything that comes in, but it's gone very quickly. Imagine an array of characters like those in Figure 2-5.

Figure 2-5. How Many of These Letters Could You Remember on an Instantaneous Exposure?

```
XMDP
CYLT
WGNR
EVOS
```

If I flashed it up really quickly and then hid it, you'd be hard pressed to be able to recall them all before they'd been forgotten; perhaps you could remember three or four.

Figure 2-6. How Many Letters *of One Row* Could You Remember on an Instantaneous Exposure?

1. X M D P
2. C Y L T
3. W G N R
4. E V O S

But if I instead ask you to remember only one row, indicated by a number between 1 and 4, you'd likely be able to remember three or four accurately in that row *regardless of which row you were given* (Figure 2-6). It's not that we can't access it; it's just that it disappears so quickly.

Channels

Note that there are different channels for different types of information being processed. We can demonstrate the two differences with a simple experiment (known as the Stroop test, from the originator). In the original, we give you a series of words made up of color names (red, blue, green). They're colored on the screen. We ask you to respond with the color of the word—that is, not what it says, but the color of the font. We do this under two conditions. First, we have the colors match the color word, so red is written in a red font. Then, we do another series where the color word is mismatched with the font color. Again, you're asked to respond with the font color.

In this book, we'll use a non-color equivalent—the picture–word test. In Figure 2-7, we ask you to name the picture of the animal shown.

Figure 2-7. Name the Animal *Pictured* Here

Now, try it again (Figure 2-8).

Figure 2-8. Name the Animal *Pictured* Here

Did you notice it was harder to do the latter image? When the word doesn't match with the image, your ability to respond with the animal name is slower. Why? Because the word itself is automatically being processed by your system, as is the image, but they interfere. Thus, we can facilitate, or hinder, comprehension by the choices we make.

Sensory Specificity

Audio is slightly different, because it is more linear (by nature). It's slower, but it's similarly of relatively short duration without some extra work. And that work is part of the next steps in the system.

There's no process involved, by the way. It happens automatically unless it's interfered with, such as with earplugs or eye patches. Then, of course, there are the aforementioned limitations of color blindness, partial or full blindness, or deafness or other hearing disorders.

Attention, Attention!

What brings information from sensory store to our conscious thinking is the process of attention (Figure 2-9). This process is limited. Have you ever tried to listen to a particular conversation in a noisy room, or pick one small image out of a swath of similar ones? Attention requires effort.

Figure 2-9. Attention and Working Memory

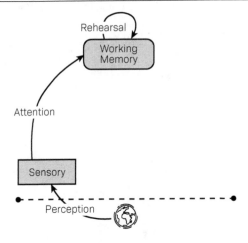

And, attention is (largely) volitional, that is, under conscious control. We can choose to watch TV, or read a book. We can switch attention from one thing to another (with some overhead; multitasking isn't really a thing). And we can largely tune out commercials on television or radio, focusing our attention. However, there's a catch.

It's not *fully* under conscious control, as the famous "cocktail party phenomena" demonstrates. Imagine you're at a party, and in a conversation with one or two other people. You're focused. However, if another group happens to mention your name, your attention is distracted *even though you weren't following their conversation*. (This also illustrates how rich your sensory store can be.) Highly salient words, like your name or the word *sex* (titter), can capture your attention. So can volume changes, pauses, and other tricks. (The advertising industry has spent considerable effort on understanding this.)

Note that attention is *not* limited to eight or any other number of seconds. The original "attention span of a goldfish" meme can be traced back to a misinterpretation of other data. Just think of an instance when a novel, movie, or game made the time fly by. Our attention is part of our cognitive architecture, which has evolved over thousands of years. It's not going to change that fast!

This also means, by the way, that our learners need support in guiding their attention. While our attention span hasn't changed, there are lots more opportunities for distraction, for one. We have so many additional channels for disturbance: social media, texts, images, and more. We also have a greater awareness of how to distract people (for better or worse). Marketers are using more sophisticated programming to capture our attention with updates and notifications. Our job, then, is to help learners filter out unnecessary distractions and know *where* to point their attention.

> **Learning:** We need to help learners focus. Remove distractions that can add to cognitive load. If the ability to perform with noise or stress is part of the context, get the processing down first, then add in the extraneous factors. Second, help learners direct their attention appropriately. Integrate labels into diagrams, and use pointers or spread out messages to introduce things one by one.

Working on Memory

The process of attention takes information from sensory store into what's called "working memory." (It's also known as short-term memory, or STM.) Working memory is what we're attending to and holding consciously in mind. This is where our conscious awareness resides. And working memory has some interesting features.

For one, it's quite limited. George Miller famously characterized the capacity of short-term memory as 7±2. For learning purposes, it's better to assume 3±1, because we don't want to step over the worst-case situation. For younger kids, it can be even less.

> **Learning:** Don't overload working memory. Keep the amount of information being processed at a low level. This includes contextual and conceptual knowledge. We can overload the system easily.

Further, that capacity is volatile. We keep information in working memory via a process of *rehearsal*, repeating it consciously, otherwise it can atrophy quickly. Or what we're thinking about can be interfered with by something else that draws our attention, effectively replacing what was there. One of the mean tricks you can play on someone makes this clear. When someone is trying to remember a new number long enough to transfer it to an address book or other form, you can interfere by reciting random numbers.

Chunking

The question then becomes, 3±1 of what? Just numbers? Here's another experiment that helps makes the case. Imagine I flash the sequence of letters in Figure 2-10 at you very briefly, and try to see how many you can recall.

Figure 2-10. How Many of These Letters Could You Remember After a Brief Exposure?

AB CTV FB IOK CI AHI

Typically, you'll be able to remember 3±1, unless one of those groupings is meaningful to you. And that's the trick. If I instead change the list not by swapping in and out letters, but instead by regrouping them, I predict that readers (from the United States, at least) will be able to remember many more or perhaps all, despite a similarly short exposure (Figure 2-11).

Figure 2-11. How Many of These Letters Could You Remember After a Brief Exposure?

ABC TV FBI OK CIA HI

What's going on here? This demonstrates chunks, which are remembered components. And it does not just apply to words; chess experts, for instance, can remember many more pieces on a board than can novices—that is, if they're in a real configuration you'd see in a chess game. Otherwise they have no advantage. What they've done is broken up chess piece configurations into meaningful chunks.

It's worth noting that chunks are aggregates of information from long-term memory triggered by the attention process from sensory memory. We see the word *car*, and if we have experience with cars, our brain activates a whole complex of information about cars that has been learned over time. We've chunked up quite a bit in that word (that is, activated quite a pattern of neural activity).

This means our brains can be more effective at working with concepts the more we aggregate them into chunks. We can think of *car* and *map* and *navigation* in one sense, instead of having *map* and *steering wheels* and *tires* and *road* and *direction* and *landmarks* and . . . too much information at once.

What this means is that working memory interacts with long-term memory. What's been brought via attention to working memory triggers chunks of prior knowledge. We have the external context, but it's represented in terms of what we comprehend. If it's not familiar, our brain will map it to what's familiar. This is partly how illusions work, our brains filling in information from long-term memory to make sense of what's being perceived. It's complicated, but the prescriptions for learning aren't.

Learning: Help learners chunk necessary information. Given that we can hold only so many bits of information, support the general building of those bits. Be very clear about what has to be in the head, and what can be in the world. And then determine explicitly what should be considered as a whole concept. We want to ensure that what's represented in short-term memory is useful based on the context.

Buckling Down for the Long-Term Memory

One thing to note from this is that, contrary to some folk beliefs, simple rehearsal does not lead to transfer to long-term memory. Rehearsal, unless there's additional processing, is unlikely to build chunks. What *does* get things into long-term memory? Elaboration. And, to get it back out, we're talking retrieval. Let's elaborate on them both (Figure 2-12).

Figure 2-12. Elaboration, Retrieval, and Long-Term Memory

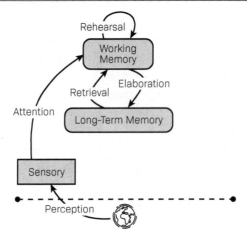

Elaboration

Elaboration is about connecting something new to something familiar. It's building upon existing knowledge. The more we process a particular new idea, the better it sticks. What we're doing essentially is activating the idea in context with other well-practiced ideas, and strengthening the relationships. Thus, when any one of the ideas is activated, we're more likely to activate these newly related ideas. So, long experience with tires and cars increases the likelihood that they'll be activated together, creating those chunks.

Processing can mean a number of things. Elaboration can be connecting it to your personal experience, to other ideas, or to things that occur in your surroundings. Ideally, it explains something in your past that was previously not understood or misunderstood. The important thing is to be developing and deepening your networks of understanding by connecting ideas together (appropriately).

Retrieval

It's not enough, of course, to store knowledge and skills. We need to be able to retrieve them from memory to use as needed. How they're stored matters. If we learn knowledge without applying it, it's unlikely to be available when needed. In cognitive science, we talk about "inert knowledge," or knowledge that's been learned and available for a test, but in a situation after the learning experience, it's not even activated.

We need to distinguish between *recognition* and *recall*. Many multiple-choice questions ask you to identify the correct response to a question rather than pull it out of memory, like a short-answer question. This is actually recognition. If we ask you to generate the response, we're asking you to recall. Recognition is a simpler, and different, task than recall. If your performance requirement is recognition, a recognition task is sufficient. However, if you really need people to be able to recall something rather than just recognize it, or more likely be able to recall and use the information, ensure that you develop the appropriate retrieval practice. That is, have learners retrieve and apply information in practice as they will need to do it in performance.

Thus, for example, there's a difference between knowing the steps of negotiation, and actually being able to conduct a negotiation. What we present to be elaborated differs, as does what we do with that information.

Retrieval, in one sense, just happens. We either recognize something, or we don't. When we're triggered by a situation, we either retrieve the right information to respond, or not. And, really, it's a probabilistic game. What we do in learning design is try to increase the probability that the information will be retrieved when and how appropriate.

Learning: We need to support encoding and retrieval. Have learners elaborate the information to explain things in their past that are related to the performance need. And provide retrieval practice in the same mode as they'll need to use it. For instance, elaborate coaching by thinking of previously observed or experienced coaching situations, and have them retrieve your coaching information to use to accomplish a coaching goal. Provide connections for learners, or support them in generating relationships between the knowledge to be learned and their preexisting knowledge.

The challenge is that we remember different things different ways. Two major types of memory have emerged, frequently labeled declarative and procedural (Figure 2-13). Declarative represents knowledge that is articulable and explicitly known. This might be the rules of the road, such as what side of the road to ride your bicycle on. Then there is implicit knowledge, often called procedural knowledge. This is knowledge that we may not be able to articulate, but manifests in what we can perform. The actual skill of riding a bike, for instance, gets developed in muscle memory. And certain reactions can be conditioned by stimuli without conscious engagement, like learning to associate a bell with food (Pavlov's famous dogs), or emotional reactions to certain songs.

Figure 2-13. Memory Types

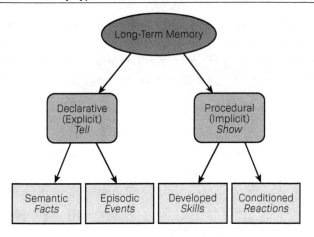

From there, declarative knowledge breaks down into two separate things to know. In the late 1970s, a number of psychologists recognized that the properties documented in our cognition didn't match up to preexisting models. Working separately, both David Rumelhart and Marvin Minsky created new models (schemas and frames, respectively) for representing declarative knowledge. In a similar way, Roger Schank created scripts for episodic knowledge in the form of events.

Both Rumelhart and Minsky were trying to account for semantic knowledge and the ways in which it manifests. One topic of consideration was how knowledge "embeds," such as how our notion of car includes wheels. Yet, wheels are also a concept on their own. Further, they were trying to account for how information is variable in different instances. For instance, we'll have bicycle concepts with different wheels from an automobile or a skateboard. An automobile-tire salesperson, however, will likely distinguish among many more facets: mud and snow, high speed, radials, and more.

On the other hand, Schank was accounting for event-based knowledge. At a particular restaurant, you sat down, ordered, paid, and were served. The fact that you paid *before* you were served was what helped him understand that he had expectations, which implied a knowledge structure. His continued research from there documented elements of the structure of events.

That also led to recognition of the power of stories. With structures like Schank's scripts, our brain can fill in information, and make our stories concise and compelling. Evidence suggests we're wired to process stories. Certainly, there are areas of the brain that respond to story. Stories make bits and pieces easier to remember and reconstruct. The information about events, episodic information, is best conveyed through story.

This means we need a structure flexible enough to accommodate this knowledge. For instance, embedding can lead to useful generalizations. On the flip side, it can lead to simplifications such as stereotyping, overgeneralizing concepts. Thus, if we need nuance, we need to ensure appropriate practice.

> **Learning:** Knowledge structures are fluid. Provide sufficient practice to ensure that an appropriate level of discrimination between concepts is present when needed.

The point here is that to learn different things, we need to use different approaches. While it's all about "doing" in the end, the type of doing may indicate different types of knowledge and support to learn it. And of course, most things we learn have more than one element. We can use declarative knowledge to guide the acquisition of procedural skills. And most performance requirements can require both declarative and episodic information.

> **Learning:** Match the instruction to the learning. The learning outcome should dictate what's an appropriate form of practice, and the necessitated knowledge in support.

Motoring On

To complete the loop, we have our motor actions (Figure 2-14). In general, we focus on three categories of motion: facial expressions, finger actions, or full-body motions. Speaking itself is a form of motor action. So are typing and mouse movements.

Figure 2-14. Control and Recognition

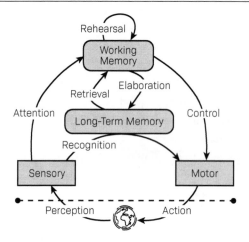

Just as there's transfer from what we perceive in learning to what we perceive in the performance environment, there's transfer from how we act on the world in the learning environment to how we are expected to perform in the world. The more we can make the learning environment require what the performance environment requires, the higher the likelihood of transfer.

Our conscious choices of action come from deliberations in working memory. This isn't to say that all actions require conscious deliberation. The nature of memory, and how we chunk information (effectively *compiling* it, in an analogy to how computer programs can get rewritten into a language for computers that's hard to understand at a semantic level), means that some things can be made automatic.

Some examples: When you first learned to tie your shoes, the act used to require considerable conscious effort, but now you can do it without thinking. Or the intention to walk happens without explicitly controlling each muscle in our legs. Similarly, the aforementioned cocktail party phenomenon triggering an attention shift happens despite our intention to focus elsewhere.

The process of situations triggering actions without conscious thought can be considered part of recognition. Here, our sensory system or higher-level intentions can allow lower-level processes to execute automatically. For instance, if someone throws you something, you might be triggered to catch it (or protect yourself) before even thinking about it. It's a conditioned response leading to a recognized behavior. This matters to the design of learning in that we want to minimize the difference between what we do in the learning experience and what we are expected to do in the world. So, reciting knowledge that came from content in bullet points is likely very different from how you're expected to apply that knowledge in a personal interaction or task execution.

> **Learning:** Make the assessment tasks mimic the real-world tasks. Even if it's via multiple choice, have the question mimic the decision one needs to make, not the knowledge one needs to make it. If that knowledge needs to be automated, do so, but then have learners apply that knowledge. Otherwise, question why it's needed.

Closing the Loop

At the end of the loop, we act on the world. We speak, move hand to keyboard or mouse, or transport ourselves to other locations. And there are consequences to that. The world may have changed on its own, and our actions can change it. It leads to potentially new sensory inputs.

This is a continuous cycle. We can break it (somewhat) by closing our eyes and meditating, for instance, and of course our active processing ceases when we sleep. Yet even then we can be triggered by outside stimulation. I reckon that an earthquake of sufficient severity, for instance, might wake someone or break meditation, or even penetrate a sensory deprivation tank.

Importantly, we're always perceiving, and there's evidence that suggests we innately try to make sense of the world. This is a topic of chapter 4. For now, however, in chapter 3 we'll look at some of the immediate artifacts of the cognitive architecture our consciousness runs on.

Activities

+ Experiment with your senses. Can you fool them with illusions? Can you interrupt your own processing? Can you condition some behavior subconsciously?

+ Consider how the phenomena discussed—attention, elaboration, chunking, retrieval—explain or predict anything you've encountered in your own experience.

+ Ensure that your practice approaches reflect the different types of memory needed to process information into learning.

+ Use the phenomena so far suggested to redesign your learning design process. What can you do differently?

CHAPTER 3

Architectural Artifacts

- The cognitive artifacts important for learning
- How we process media

When you learn a new skill, you may hear certain mantras repeated. In tennis or baseball, you may hear "Swing *through* the ball." In physics, it's "Draw the forces." In learning design, you may hear "Manage the cognitive load." The point is that the instructors are not thinking about the underpinning cognitive architecture; instead, they're thinking about the thinking and learning that runs *on* the architecture. And, our architecture leads to some artifacts that are important in designing learning.

Thus, we've got to account for how to present information, what to present, how much to present, and more. We need to be careful about what we have learners do, when, and know what helps and hinders. These are the core factors that influence what learning design can and should address.

Phenomenal Learning

While there are lots of artifacts of our architecture, only a subset is critical for learning. Those are the ones we'll cover here. First, we'll look at ones that affect the learning process, including practice and feedback effects, and supporting elements like models and examples. We'll subsequently look at media properties.

Feedback

The previous chapter covered the importance of both elaboration and retrieval. For retrieval to be effective, we need to know whether what we retrieved led us to the correct outcome or not. More importantly, we need to know why and how we were wrong, so we can change our approach the next time. In essence, we need feedback. Feedback lets our brain know whether or not to strengthen the relationship. If we get it wrong, we don't want to reward whatever choice we made. And we need specific clues about just *how* we went wrong, and what we should do instead. While "right/wrong" feedback can, over sufficient time, allow our pattern-matching to learn the correct relationships, better feedback accelerates the process.

Mirjam Neelen and Paul Kirschner, in their book *Evidence-Informed Learning Design*, summarize research and point to three types of feedback: corrective, directive, and epistemic. Corrective feedback merely indicates what's wrong and what to do instead. This is like the types of e-learning software that have one feedback response for all the wrong choices. Directive feedback goes further and says *why* the action was the wrong choice. Because of our tendency to make patterned mistakes based upon misconceptions, this is the minimum you should provide. Note that it requires separate answers for each response. Finally, epistemic feedback asks learners why their answer might be wrong, not correcting them but guiding them to the answer. The latter leads to the best long-term outcomes, but is harder to build in without a graduated feedback mechanism.

Valerie Shute, in a whitepaper, nicely summarized other research on feedback. Here we focus on the key elements that provide the most value in achieving learning outcomes.

For one, the feedback should be about the learner's performance, *not the learner*. That is, don't make it personal about their strengths and weaknesses, but instead focus on how they did in this instance, and what can be better.

Feedback should also be clear, specific, and minimal. Include no extra material other than that which relates the actual performance to the desired one, and why. There shouldn't be praise or blame, merely an accurate accounting of how this went right or wrong.

Also, feedback should be delayed until the performer is done performing. Interrupting them can interfere with the opportunity to learn. Feedback can be delayed for simple things, relative to the learner's capability. That is, delay feedback when the learner's expertise is high. However, for complex tasks, immediate feedback is useful.

> **Learning:** Feedback should be impersonal, clear, minimal, and delivered upon completion of the practice. It should not only provide the outcome, but also explain why the answer was wrong and what would be correct.

Models

A fundamental feature of our brains is that they're pattern-matchers and meaning-makers. We look for stories about why things happen. This made sense evolutionarily; it allowed us to explain what's happened and predict what will happen. It also means that we don't remember rote information or large amounts of abstract information very well. We need to account for this in our designs.

Our brains naturally build models that explain outcomes. These models are conceptual and contain causal relationships that tie input to outcome. We use them to explain or predict outcomes. This is useful because when we can predict the outcomes of different actions, we can choose the best outcome. And they can therefore be used to explain why a decision was wrong, as feedback.

Thus, models are a valuable component of feedback, because they explain the "why." You want people to use models to guide their decisions, and you want to explicitly develop models for people, incorporate them in your design, and use them as a basis for feedback.

For example, in an insightful experiment, David Kieras and Susan Bovair gave a diagram and instructions to two different groups. The first group received a control panel and explicit instructions for how to use it (Figure 3-1). Paraphrasing, they were told to:

+ Flip the SP switch and verify that the SP indicator lights.
+ When the EB and MA indicators light, flip the ES Selector to MA.
+ Press the FM button, and verify that the PF indicator lights.

They were trained until they could perform this task reliably and repeatedly.

Figure 3-1. Control Panel

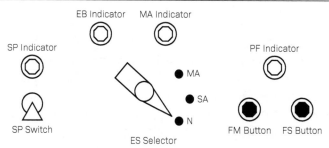

A second group got a model that included the same controls, but this time it had a mental model associated with it (Figure 3-2). Here, they were told these were the controls for the phaser banks of the starship USS *Enterprise*. Their instructions were slightly different:

+ Flip the ship's power switch to turn on power, and charge the Energy Booster.

+ When the Energy Booster and Main Accumulator indicators are lit, set the Energy Source Selector to the Main Accumulator.

+ Press the Fire Main button and verify that the phasers have fired via the Phaser Firing Indicator.

And, again, they were trained to reliably and repeatedly perform the task.

Figure 3-2. Mental Model Panel

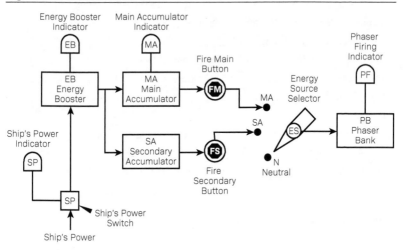

The nonmodel group with just the control panel took slightly less time to learn and performed slightly more reliably. But then the experimenters made a change. They broke the connection between the Energy Booster and the Main Accumulator (conceptually) and asked both groups to figure out how to still light the PF indicator. The group trained on the control panel struggled, while the mental model group pretty reliably flipped the Energy Source Selector to the Secondary Accumulator, and pressed the Fire Secondary button. And, as the model predicted, the Phaser Firing Indicator worked.

The important lesson here is that models give us a basis to adapt when things go wrong or when contexts are variable. Mental models provide the basis for making decisions. They have to be the *right* sort of models to support inferences and predictions, but most everything we ask people to do has a reason. What we have to do is help learners understand those models, and give them a basis to cope in uncertainty, which is typically (and increasingly) the case.

Another artifact of our cognitive architecture is that if the model we build isn't accurate, we don't look to replace it. Instead, we patch it. Given that the core is unlikely to be fundamentally changed, this means that a bad model will persist. For natural situations this is apt, but for more complex learning, this suggests the necessity of good models to begin with.

Think about sports. We use explicit metaphors like "Grip the racket/sword/bat like you're shaking a hand." We're using metaphors as models to communicate guidance. We internalize this advice, over time, into our practiced approaches.

Interestingly, multiple models may help, and they may even be necessary. Rand Spiro, in creating his Cognitive Flexibility Theory, used a case study about learning how muscle fibers operate. He found that using a sculling or rowing metaphor wasn't enough, and it took multiple iterations to lead to accurate inferences.

Also, most of our mistakes don't come from random responses. Though there is some randomness in our architecture (it's evolutionarily adaptive), our mistakes instead tend to be patterned ("No matter what I do, they still . . ."). They come from bringing in models that seem appropriate but aren't a good match. Stereotypes are one phenomena that exhibits faulty models in action.

> **Learning:** Present models of causal relationships that provide a basis for predictions and explanations. Use them in examples and in feedback on practice.

Misconceptions

As we've covered, most mistakes are patterned, representing a few common ways to misunderstand the material. That is, mistakes don't tend to be random. We can call those misinterpretations *misconceptions*, and they're important for learning design.

Learners bring with them models they're familiar with from other areas or other experiences. These models make sense, but they might not be appropriate in the current situation. Say, for instance, a novice customer-service agent might think that the right first step with a customer complaint is to resolve it, instead of acknowledging the emotional impact and apologizing.

There is some randomness in our architecture, to be sure. It's an evolutionary advantage because if some of those random actions happen to be better, they'll be rewarded and gradually become part of an improved repertoire of action. This, however, is a slow approach, and we're interested in a more rapid and principled improvement.

In a learning situation, however, we can view these typical errors as not just a problem, but an opportunity. They give us the necessary alternatives to the right answer. We can identify and address them in the learning experience instead of having to deal with them in the performance situation. And we can counter each wrong belief with feedback specific to learners having made that mistake. It's valuable then to use models in the feedback to provide the opportunity for continuing improvement.

> **Learning:** Use the misconceptions people have in your learning design. Make your alternatives to the right answer common ways that people get it wrong. And address each mistaken approach individually.

Context

People perform better in retrieving information during concrete tasks than abstract ones. Working on problems that are comprehensible and grounded in real situations (even if made up) tend to be recalled better than abstract problems. For instance, the math on dimensions of a building (How many square feet of carpet would you need for a room that's five feet by six feet?) would be more likely to be retained than math for abstract problems (What's the product of 5 × 6?).

The action loop that is invoked in cognition starts with the stimuli that is the focus of attention. Relevant prior knowledge plays a role in interpreting the signals into what gets represented in short-term memory. Our interpretation of the context guides our decisions about actions to take. We predict the outcomes of different actions as a way to assess the likely consequences and act accordingly.

Context also determines our space of transfer. Think of the contexts we see as a space covering all the possible correct and incorrect applications. If we keep our focus narrow, our transfer won't be as broad as if we pick contexts from a representative sample. Some tasks have only "near" transfer requirements, that is we only need to transfer to very similar situations. Others are "far," in that the transfer requirements can be to situations that are quite different but still relevant. They also have different requirements for contextual practice.

Figure 3-3. Context and Transfer

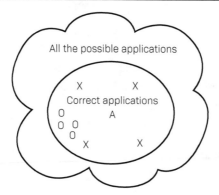

So, in the hypothetical space portrayed in Figure 3-3, we're more likely to transfer to situation A if we've seen examples in the contexts labeled X than if we pick the ones labeled O. For example, if we're looking at negotiation, and all the examples and practice are in contexts of working with suppliers (O), you might not transfer to situations dealing with negotiating with your boss about a raise (A). If, however, you also practice negotiation for sale prices, employee policies, and more (X), you're more likely to transfer to salary, and even to home situations such as purchasing a suite of furniture or this year's family retreat.

A further element is that we perform better in concrete contexts, as opposed to abstract ones. That is, real problems lead to better retention and transfer than ones that are decontextualized. To make this concrete, let's look at two tasks. In both, we're given a rule governing the relationships between what's on one side of a piece of paper and the other. For the first, we're told that there's a character on one side, and a digit on the other. The rule is that if the letter is a vowel, the number must be odd. And, we are to determine which of the four examples we need to turn over to ensure that the rule is not violated (Figure 3-4).

Figure 3-4. A Sample Task

The rule is: If the letter on one side is a vowel, then the digit must be odd. Which of these would you have to turn over to ensure the rule isn't violated?

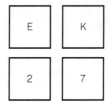

Now let's do a similar task. Here, the rule is that if the amount on one side of a check is more than fifty dollars, there must be a signature on the other side. Again, your task is to determine which of the four examples would need to be turned over to ensure that the rule is not violated (Figure 3-5).

Figure 3-5. A Similar Sample Task

The rule is: If the amount on the front is more than $50, then there must be a signature on the other side. Which of these would you have to turn over to ensure the rule isn't violated?

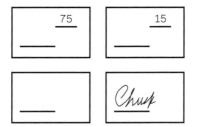

These two examples are functionally equivalent. The correct answer in both cases are the left-most choices: The "E" and "2" cards, and the "75" and no signature cards (checks, of course). And if you're like most people, you might get the first wrong but do much better on the second (if you get them independently). Why? The first is exactly the same, formally.

The fact is that we perform better when the example is concrete, as opposed to abstract. And we retain and transfer better as well. This holds true for abstract math problems through to sales techniques. Examples should be concrete, even if simplified.

Learning: Choose an appropriate suite of concrete contexts, spread across examples and practice, to support the needed transfer, near or far.

Cognitive Load

A frequent interfering factor in learning is overloading the capacity of working memory. If the task has too many additional details that aren't essential, it can overwhelm our mental resources. John Sweller's work on cognitive load talks about germane, or intrinsic, versus extraneous load. For instance, if we're asking learners to understand how to change a tire, giving too much data about the history of cars could overwhelm their working memory and reduce their comprehension of the necessary process.

Figure 3-6. Cognitive Load

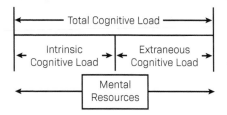

What the diagram in Figure 3-6 shows is that there are only so many cognitive resources. The total load is composed of germane details and extraneous ones. We want to keep the extra load to a minimum, or we can overload learners' ability to process the information. We help learners by chunking up information and having them automate it, to reduce the load. Most important, we need to be conscious of the load. When we present the "nice to know" as well as the "need to know," we can be providing too much.

Thus, we want to remove irrelevant details. Yet we also want to maintain relevant details, including context. This is one of the reasons testing and refining designs is important, because it can be possible to over- or underestimate the demands of a task. Testing and refining is a necessary component of design.

Among the prescriptions to reduce cognitive load includes putting labels into diagrams, instead of having letters that you have to look up the meaning of. The need to mentally integrate the labels adds extraneous load (Figure 3-7). Similarly, so does adding extraneous details to diagrams, images, or text.

Figure 3-7. Additional Cognitive Load

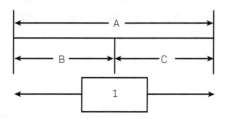

A. Total Cognitive Load   1. Mental Resources
B. Intrinsic Cognitive Load
C. Extraneous Cognitive Load

Learning: Ensure that the task requirements, with all the elements, are within the learner's reach (if not their grasp). Test to ensure that the requirements don't exceed learner capability.

Automation

The more we reprocess the same knowledge, the more automated it gets. Our knowledge gets increasingly compiled away from conscious to subconscious memory, inaccessible for inspection. Think of describing how you tie your shoe; it's challenging to communicate because it's so automated. As a consequence, experts literally can't tell you about 70 percent of what they do, as documented by the Cognitive Technology group at the University of Southern California!

Also, the intent to put on one's shoes usually includes tying the laces without conscious intervention. Or we might brake for trouble while driving even before we recognize the threat. Thus, pilots are trained such that they're liable to react appropriately before they even consciously process the problem and the appropriate response.

Automating certain tasks through memorization, like knowing our multiplication tables, makes other things easier. We automate what we need to, leaving our minds free to focus on the important things. What's automated happens quickly and effortlessly. What's conscious is slow and effortful. We should aim to automate (either mentally or through technology) what we don't want to have to work on, so we can choose the problems we want to do.

Learning: Support appropriate automatization. This is like the previous recommendation to support chunking, but here it's about taking those designed chunks and ensuring sufficient practice and feedback to support taking the use of the chunks from conscious to rote.

The way we retrieve learning matters. What we're doing with information in practice is what we'll be able to do with it in a performance situation. Asking people to identify knowledge in the form of discriminating among different answers is a far cry from being asked to make decisions based upon different criteria. Don't ask for recognition when recall and application is what is needed.

Primed for Action

Given that learning is activating relevant patterns together, strengthening the relationship, another phenomenon emerges. Responses can be "primed" by activating related material. Thus, if you're responding to a question about whether a sequence of letters is a word, a previous word from the same domain will activate related concepts and speed your response. Thus, to identify if *nurse* is a word, preceding the question with the word *doctor* will increase how quickly you can determine it's a word (Figure 3-8).

Figure 3-8. Which One Would Be Responded to Faster if Preceded by the Word *Doctor*?

Answer, for each: Is this a word?
Nurse
Gremp
Bread

This is one of the reasons we activate relevant prior knowledge before learning. The patterns representing this knowledge are then primed for connecting. It makes learning more effective, supporting elaboration.

Learning: Retrieve in the way to be used. If people need to *use* information to make decisions, have them do that, not merely demonstrate that they know the information.

Retrieval Phenomena

One element of designing learning experiences that differs from traditional event-based learning approaches is the requirement for spaced retrieval. Know that only so much strengthening of the connections between neurons can occur at one time. The process that strengthens the connections gets fatigued, and basically needs sleep before more strengthening can occur. It's worth looking at the implications of that. Will Thalheimer summarized the results in his report "Spacing Learning Events Over Time" (Figure 3-9).

Figure 3-9. Spacing Effects

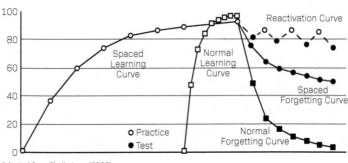

Adapted from Thalheimer (2006).

The normal forgetting curve, made famous by Hermann Ebbinghaus's research on random words, which we saw in chapter 1, shows a sharp decline. This is when there's massed practice. You'll do well on a test, but it'll be gone only a few days later. (This often characterizes the college experience.) However, if you space learning out over time, it's retained better. Strengthening information processing sufficient to survive a time delay requires spacing.

Reactivation acts like further spacing. Just how much practice and spacing depends on the inherent complexity of the material, the importance of getting it right, and how frequently it's actually used in performance. Things that are important and complex but used infrequently may need lots of practice. Think of the hours in simulators pilots expend for situations they hope never to face!

Learning: Space learning out over time. Massed practice in an event model isn't likely to lead to sufficient retention. Build spaced practice into your learning model, and into your design process.

In addition to spacing out learning, another robust phenomenon about retrieval practice is the benefit of varied practice over massed practice. It turns out that mixing in practice of other elements before seeing more of the same also facilitates retention.

That is, if you're studying A, B, and C, you'll do better with a practice schedule looking something like:

ABACBABCACBC

Rather than:

AAAABBBBCCCC

So, for instance, if we're developing data analytics skills, we might follow a problem about data collection with data-cleaning practice. Then, the next day, we might do another data-cleaning exercise, but follow it with a data collection activity. And then we might go back and do a design activity before moving on to another data collection task and then data-cleaning practice again. The goal is to gradually advance everything, but mix it up to build in spacing and unpredictability. The ideal spacing is to have practice right before the learning is likely to atrophy.

It's more than just spacing; it's retrieving in situations where you're not sure what you're going to be asked. When you struggle to retrieve in uncertain conditions, you're mimicking more accurately what performance environments are liable to be like.

A related element addresses just what you should be practicing *now*. In his book *Peak*, Anders Ericsson pointed out the necessity of what he called "deliberate" practice. That is, what you practice has to be right thing for where you are. It's not just practice; it has to be focused on the next element in your skill progression. It's about adding the right next complexity to your development. In tennis, if you've mastered the swing and follow-through for an accurate hit, maybe it's time to develop your placement. And in customer service, after you've mastered the trouble-shooting procedure, maybe it's about dealing with customer emotions.

Another dimension to this is what Robert Bjork has referred to as "desirable difficulty." Here, the focus in on not just what skill is next, but the right level of ability. It has to be the right next thing and the right level of it. We'll look at this again when we talk about the emotional aspects of learning.

Learning: If you can, mix up the practice and manage challenge level. Switch from this element to that, which helps make it less predictable. Try to make the challenge level appropriate for where the learner is.

Scaffolding

How can we simplify problems that seem to incorporate too much for learners at one time? We have a number of types of support that we can provide, which we often call "scaffolding." The metaphor is that of the support around a building under construction that is gradually removed.

One method is making problems initially simpler, with no complications. For instance, you may recall solving math problems where the numbers were whole and round, and when multiplied or divided similarly resulted in round numbers. This allows the focus to be on the steps involved, and not the computational aspects. Of course, then we use more realistic numbers to support transfer.

Similarly, we may not involve complexities initially. In a game I developed on project management for engineers, which also included a goal of being easy to work with, the first few times, you dealt with easygoing engineers. After a few tries to get the mechanics down, then you had to deal with more difficult personality types.

We can also have part of the task already completed for the learner, initially. The learner gradually takes on more and more responsibility. In apprenticeships, learners often start out doing peripheral tasks like fetching and setup, while they learn the overall task and context.

What you're doing is managing the challenge and cognitive load in ways that learners can cope with. You let them develop their chunks and then test them in more and more robust settings, gradually moving them to full performance.

From Artifacts to Media Effects

We've looked at a variety of outcomes of our architecture that affect learning. These have to do with the content and actions. A separate set of them can be characterized as media effects, or how that content is presented and processed. Let's take a look.

Media Matters

One result of our information-processing system is how we comprehend media. Given that using communication is the core way we transcend the need for each of us to either adapt evolutionarily or learn things on our own, the ability to optimize the clarity of material is critical. The development of language at all is the only thing more critical than the development of written language. Consequently, reading and writing are critical cognitive skills. Similarly, mathematics is the third "R" (reading, writing, and 'rithmetic), and all three are considered core to the ability to function as an adult.

Writing

For instruction, there are meaningful ways to ensure that your writing is read. In addition to the cognitive load issue, some visual elements assist in comprehension, such as highlighting and spacing, which tap into our ability to make detailed visual discriminations. Patti Shank has done a marvelous job of translating many learning science elements into her Make It Learnable series of books; the one on reading is particularly good guidance here.

Highlighting is one area that isn't utilized sufficiently for learners. Using italics, boldface, underlining, and other emphasis indicators can help learners notice what's important. To a limit, of course; text that's too visually busy is also problematic.

A second element is white space. Indents, bullets, breaks between paragraphs, and more are all tools to help manage the chunking of information. The flip side is to work to make manageable chunks instead of monolithic blocks of text.

A third element is style. Writing in the first person and in the reader's language is critical for communication. A conversational style is recommended over formal language, as is active voice over passive (which I struggle with, mea culpa; hurray for editors!). Mobile learning initially drove my own emphasis on brevity, but it's reinforced in web design as well.

Jakob Nielsen has written on writing for the web, emphasizing the previous elements. Reading from a screen typically is slower than reading on paper, so e-learning needs less text. Full sentences aren't always necessary; phrases can be sufficient. And this is true for all learning, whether delivered digitally or in print. We tend to overwrite.

> **Learning:** Take a second pass at your writing to trim it!

Media

One final point: dramatic writing emphasizes "Show, don't tell." The implication here is to use visuals when possible. This does not mean gratuitous graphics (which can increase cognitive load), but instead having diagrams to explain complicated conceptual relationships, and images to convey context. Connie Malamed explored the implications of visuals for learning in her 2015 book *Visual Design Solutions*.

In Donald Norman's *Things That Make Us Smart*, the sequel to his classic *Design of Everyday Things* (the latter is a must-read for anyone who designs for people; how many books will truly change the way you see the world?), he shows an example of a complex piece of text:

> They found that while subjects would rate the analogies, from best to worst, as literally similar, true analogy, mere appearance, and false analogy, their recall for stories, from best to worst, was literally similar, mere appearance, true analogy, and false analogy.

He then mentions how a graphic can make this much clearer (Figure 3-10).

Figure 3-10. Mapping Graphic

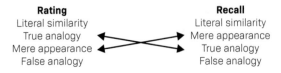

Here, the differences between the two elements are clearer. (He was kind enough not to mention in the book that the turgid prose was from my thesis draft, and that it was his recommendation to add the graph, which of course ultimately appeared in the final document!) The important point here is to use the right media for the message.

In general, the properties of media matter. One important additional dimension is dynamism. For things that change over time, such as processes or systems, you may need dynamic media, as opposed to static representations (Figure 3-11).

Figure 3-11. Media Matters

	Static	Dynamic
Contextual	Photo	Video
Conceptual	Graphic	Animation
Linguistic	Text	Speech

For context, photos or videos contain the actual setting. Similar to a story, we can fill in much from seeing it. So, you might show a picture of a piece of equipment or a video of some action. When you want to strip away context and focus on the concepts, you can use graphics or animations (dynamic graphics), like Figure 3-11. Here we're mapping conceptual information onto spatial information. And, when processing dynamic visuals, such as a video or an animated diagram, spoken annotation allows the auditory channel to communicate language, rather than overloading the visual channel with text to complement the visuals. Imagine trying to read text accompanying a video at the same time! While we may do this with closed captioning, remember that we're losing part of the signal because our brains are working to infer what's happening visually while we read the prose.

These guidelines aren't hard and fast. For instance, Ken Burns has used narrated sequences of static images to tell a story both because of a lack of video at the time but also because it communicates narrative. Text linking images together can tell a story, and so can narration of the images, or a dynamic video. Story is a dynamic way to communicate examples *and* to bring in context as well.

And, slightly on a soapbox, comics, graphic novels, animations (animated diagrams), and cartoons can be used to combine both context and concept as well. I think they're underused and powerful, because of that combination across boundaries, as well as some other, more pragmatic features. For one, they're low bandwidth, relatively speaking at least. They're also easy to globalize and localize, because they're a part of popular culture in most every country. And they can work well with low-literacy populations, using visuals to communicate what otherwise might need to be written. Kevin Thorn is exploring comics more for use in learning and instruction.

> **Learning:** In general, use the right media for the message. You can mix it up to maintain variety for novelty's sake, but don't undermine the essential message. And consider comic or graphic-novel formats.

Activities

- Based upon the artifacts discussed in this chapter, prioritize the smallest changes to your design process that can give you biggest impact in your outcomes, and implement them.
- Evaluate your learning design to ensure you're not creating an overwhelming cognitive load.
- Create a mechanism to get and develop models that will actually guide learners in performance.
- Similarly, create a mechanism to determine the least number of contexts, across examples and practice, that will give you the best transfer.
- Given the requirements for spacing, variety, and desirable difficulty in practice, find a way to extend your learning experiences beyond the training event.

CHAPTER 4

Emergent Cognition

- New frameworks from cognitive science
- Social learning

Evidence mounts that people are not as logical as we would like to believe. This might not seem to matter to us, but consider that we're designing to achieve successful performance. If our learners don't act in the ways we imagine, our outcomes might not match our intents. Thus, it's worth exploring some more recent frameworks that provide new insights into how we really think, and considering the implications for designing to achieve effective outcomes.

That story of stores and processes and artifacts in chapters 2 and 3 pretty much characterizes the basics of cognition. However, in addition to the artifacts mentioned previously, we also have these emergent phenomena: situated, distributed, social, and the free energy principle. These emergent properties have implications for what we do.

Without a Net

As a start, it helps to realize a cognitive revolution that occurred in two separate, but related, initiatives. The first one was a revelation from a previously mentioned researcher, David Rumelhart, and his colleague Jay McClelland. The second was the resulting situated cognition movement.

Rumelhart recognized that the behavior he was trying to account for with his schema approach wasn't well captured in the formal, logic-based computational models that were then being used. He was looking for an architecture that could more naturally accommodate the variations from formal reasoning that are seen empirically.

He ended up with what are now known as neural net or connectionist models, which he and McClelland termed "parallel distributed processing." These models could learn to do simple categorization tasks, and made mistakes more like how humans did.

These models now form the basic approach of much of machine learning, where you don't code the relationships formally, but instead use sets of data to train the networks to perform. Yet for now, that's not the right level of analysis for how humans learn, as we covered at the beginning of the previous chapter. However, the ways in which these models performed helped spark the awareness of the situated nature of our cognition.

Situating Thinking

When we act in the world, the expectation is that we'll do an appropriate analysis, consciously evaluate the alternatives, and make a rational decision. However, that's not very accurate. Given that this is the case, how *do* we make good decisions? We need to understand the biases before we can answer that question. The connectionist approach helped show that our thinking is much more situated in our context.

As Andy Clark let us know in *Being There: Putting Brain, Body, and World Together Again*, our cognition isn't principled, but instead emerges out of the interaction between our memory and our current context. Our thoughts about a dog will be very different after an experience with a cute cuddly one versus one that lunged at you through a fence and barked aggressively. Similarly, we'll think differently after an advertisement extolling a particular point of view or showing an emotionally compelling experience.

Much of what we think we perceive is actually filled in by our memory. Our situational understanding is colored by the context as well as by formal principle. Illusions work, for instance, by drawing upon the way our brains fill in gaps (Figure 4-1). Recognizing this is important for understanding how we act in the world. We need to account for how our brains complete things and how we may act differently in different situations, including those that we might rationally comprehend as essentially the same situation.

Figure 4-1. An Impossible Image

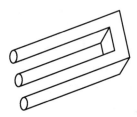

This is important when we're performing *and* when we're developing the capability to perform. So, for instance, if we can be swayed by a current context, some structure may benefit us in keeping us on track. We have a variety of tools to accommodate the gaps in our cognitive architecture. For instance, Atul Gawande, in *The Checklist Manifesto*, makes the case for how checklists support many types of performance. By externalizing information by creating a list of items to keep in mind, we're acknowledging the flaws in our ability to remember rote information and providing scaffolding for success.

It also means that if we want performance that's principled, we have to enable learners to perform across contexts. And if we want the appropriate contextual response, we have to develop that. As we discussed in the previous chapter, we generalize across what we experience. And, we're liable not to transfer beyond that. Thus, to support appropriate transfer and contextualization, we should be exposed to (a representative sample of) the spacing of appropriate application.

We also aren't formal, logical reasoners, in general. As Daniel Kahneman lets us know in *Thinking, Fast and Slow*, we have two systems, and mostly rely on the quick, intuitive one that makes snap decisions (Figure 4-2). This is fine for areas in which we have expertise, having compiled relevant knowledge. The second system is more conscious and logical, and also effortful and therefore harder to invoke. We often use the rational system to justify the decisions we make with the first system! And, more important, we can use the fast system inappropriately when it's not the right solution. We are liable to overgeneralize our expertise rather than invest the appropriate mental effort. Hence the need for instruction.

Figure 4-2. Kahneman's Two Systems

Fast	Slow
Subconscious	Conscious
Fast	Slow
Easy	Effortful

Thus, we tend to resort to simple algorithms and avoid complex work. In the previous chapter, when we talked about the context and concrete versus abstract, we used the examples of turning over cards to determine if a rule is violated. One example was abstract and one was concrete. It's likely that what's happening in the former case is that rather than do the mental computation, subjects are keying into a simple heuristic that uses the keywords in the rule, *even* and *consonant*. Whereas in the latter case, with the check value and the need to sign, most subjects likely have real-world knowledge that makes using the example's knowledge to make the decision easier. Thus, we need to ensure that we provide sufficient information, via models and practice, to support appropriate inferences or to trigger conscious processing.

We should look to automate what should be triggered and provide sufficient practice across contexts to support appropriate transfer. We can't stick with just a few bullet points and think we'll get appropriate outcomes. We need to envision the situations in which the knowledge is relevant, anticipate ways in which learners can go astray, and ensure that they have the chance to correct course *before* it counts.

There's also the Dunning-Kruger effect, which states that people with a low level of knowledge about some topic overestimate their actual understanding. It's a case of not having enough knowledge to know that you don't have the knowledge! In practice, the more someone learns about a topic, the more they realize they don't know. Again, we're *not* formal reasoners. And we should help people know the limitations of what we're assisting them with, so they don't mistakenly overgeneralize.

The implications here are first to provide support for reasoning that isn't natural to us. In addition, we need to automate the right decisions with sufficient practice.

Learning: The situated nature of our cognition means we can be prone to insufficiently transfer knowledge from one context to another. So, in addition to sufficient practice to support retention, we also need to consider the contexts of practice. We want to ensure that our practice contexts span the space of applicability—that is, cover all the situations we want the learner to apply the knowledge in. The practice contexts don't have to cover every situation, but instead cover sufficient breadth so that we'll appropriately transfer to those situations we didn't see in practice.

Thinking Outside the Box

In *Cognition in the Wild*, Ed Hutchins paints a picture that contradicts the old cognitive model. The general conception was that thinking was all in the head, but his research on ship navigation helped show that our thinking is distributed around the world. He showed how we use time signals, angles, and maps to create successful navigation. And we see that cognition is distributed in many ways; we use documents like spreadsheets and drawing tools as externalizations that couple with our brains to accomplish things that would be impossible all in our heads.

Our brains, with limited working memory, are not able to keep in mind all the elements and relationships that exist. By placing them in the world, in a variety of mechanisms such as mathematical models or diagrams, we reduce our cognitive load, which allows us to process small pieces at a time without losing the overall context.

Note that these tools can be simple, like chalkboards or whiteboards, or as complex as 3D visualizations. For that matter, it can be 3D printers or other physical tools that replicate the work environment. Performance support, as an alternative to instruction, is predicated on the ability to put information in the world to reduce the requirement for putting information into the head.

These external representations and interactions are important. While our brains are good at certain things, like pattern-matching, model-building, and meaning-making, they're really bad at retaining rote and arbitrary information, particularly large quantities thereof. And we're bad at performing rote operations reliably. As mentioned, there's some randomness built into our system.

Digital technology is the exact opposite. We've developed tools to compensate for our limitations. Things like checklists, lookup tables, and decision trees have been used for centuries to keep track of information we're unable to maintain in our brain. Digital tools like calculators and other interactive representations like word processing have extended that capability. Together we're far more formidable than either alone (Figure 4-3).

This is important to think about in designing solutions both for ourselves and others. We can try to put information in our heads, or in the world. As pointed out, putting rote information into our heads is hard. So we should ask ourselves, as designers, what can be in the world? What can we externalize? The tools I've mentioned can keep us on track and represent things we struggle with.

Figure 4-3. Distributed Cognition

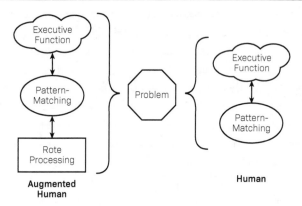

Thus, we should design solutions so that we have the proper mix between what we do well and what tools do well. And, we should design the support and then design the training to go along. I call it backwards design (Figure 4-4). That is, start with the end in mind and work backwards, similar to Grant Wiggins and Jay McTighe's *Understanding by Design*, but including the tools as well as the learning. The core elements are:

+ What would the ideal performance look like?
+ Let's design the tool part of it.
+ Finish by designing learning that incorporates the tool.

The goal, to maximize success and minimize learning, is to put as much as possible in the world first, and *then* decide what goes in the head. For instance, when writing another book, I created the performance support tools first, before determining what I should explain to make the overall outcome maximally effective and efficient. Similarly, I decided to include the "learning" pieces before I started writing out all of my thoughts.

Learning: Don't put in your head what can be in the world. Our brains are very bad at remembering large quantities of information, particularly if it's arbitrary, and similarly bad at complex calculations. Digital technology is the reverse. We should determine what can be in the world first, and then design learning to accommodate those resources.

Figure 4-4. Backward Design

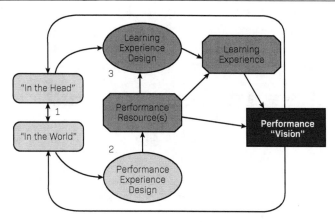

Getting Social

We're social animals. Our evolutionary advantage came from what researchers Robert Brandon and Norbert Hornstein termed *phenotypic plasticity*. What that means is that we adapt within the individual, not the species. Animals have had to evolve thicker coats to cope with an ice age, whereas we can share how to make better clothing. If we learn how to do something better, we all can benefit, and not have to rediscover it on our own.

So, after situated and distributed learning, we can extend distributed to people as well as things, and investigate the notion of social learning. The recognition that we use external representations came from observations of teams using maps and clocks to synchronize action and capture representations—multiple people as well as representations. There's a growing recognition that our value is not just what we know, but also *whom* we know.

A key focus for thinking about the benefits of social learning is investigating the differences in processing between how you see things and how others do. In the individual case of presenting something, you do some mental processing when you transform it from an idea to a concrete representation. (Ever think you understand something until you try to capture it, such as writing it up, and then find out you need to connect a few more elements? That's what we're talking about.)

The list goes on. If someone else looks at what you've produced, they do processing, and if they respond, they do more. If you then look at what they've created, you do more processing, and you respond even more. At the same time, the quality of the product is enriched! (This is why I blog. Feedback!) Thus, this works both for learning and for getting work done (Figure 4-5).

Figure 4-5. Interacting Around a Representation

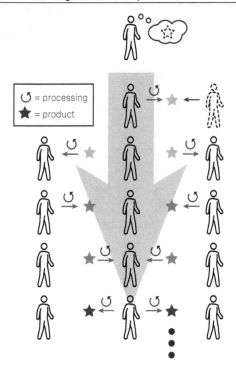

Now, if a group has an assignment to produce something together, such as a response to a problem, if everyone thinks about it separately first, there's a lot of processing happening. Then, if everyone reacts to everyone else's ideas, and works toward a shared understanding (and output), even more processing is happening. And, again, the output is better from the richer viewpoints presented in working toward the solution (Figure 4-6).

Figure 4-6. Interacting Around a Group Project

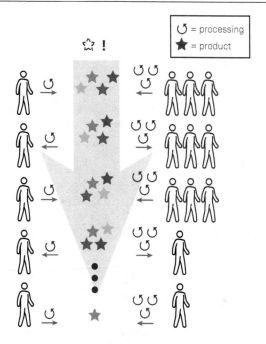

This suggests that social learning leads to both better learning and better product. There are constraints, but it suggests that at least for certain types of learning and at certain times in projects, social interaction is a benefit. When the overhead for coordinating the social work is addressed by the resolution of ambiguity, we have a case for social learning. When the likelihood for ambiguity is high, like interpreting regulations, negotiating a shared understanding may be beneficial. When the outcome is relatively straightforward, such as how to operate a particular device, there may not be as much benefit. And, of course, there are overheads in developing social learning, such as coordinating schedules. Thus, it should be used appropriately.

Another way of thinking about social learning is about learning from others. Albert Bandura, in his *Social Cognitive Theory*, posited that observing and internalizing what others do is a fundamental component of learning—in short, copying what they do. Thus, it's not only about negotiating a shared understanding, but also about seeing how concepts play out in practice. This can be through videos, but taking turns and observing others is valuable as well. Similarly, critiquing others' performances can help internalize self-monitoring, which then can lead to self-improving learners.

The recent evidence of so-called mirror neurons, or neurons that will trigger whether we're performing or watching someone else perform, suggests that observing is fundamental. My inference is that if you observe someone's performance *and it's within your range of ability*, watching them can be very beneficial in improving performance. I think observing someone doing something beyond your range can be fascinating but not useful, and observing what's already within your capability is likely boring.

> **Learning:** Use social learning activities when appropriate. That includes showing modeled examples (including the instructor modeling the behavior), and using group work when conditions are right.

A related view is that *all* learning is social. Russian psychologist Lev Vygotsky posited that we had to learn something socially before we could internalize it. His famous zone of proximal development (ZoPD), where learning happens, is the gap between what you can do easily and what you can't even with help. It's that social help in the right location where learning is generated.

For design purposes, we can make assignments to show our thinking, or even to collectively generate shared outputs. The benefits of seeing others' interpretations can help unpack misconceptions and reveal important nuances.

In one case, I was talking to an organization about a course it ran. It involved making decisions about whether certain expenditures were allowable. The existing course was a lot of bullet points and expert presentation *about* the expenditures. I opined that giving them a series of cases to negotiate, starting with black and white cases and then gradually moving to more ambiguous ones (shades of gray), would be more valuable than the course!

Learning together can be created for formal learning, and groups working together as teams can solve problems, but there's a next level. As we become practitioners in a field, we can join with other practitioners to share and advance understanding. That's commonly known as a community of practice, and is part of how we advance beyond what we've learned formally. Fostering these involves separate skills, but it is an extended way to support learning and learners.

Learning: Social learning is both powerful and costly. We need to be clear about when and how to use it. In situations like formal education, where learners are expected to regularly convene, use that time for important collaborative work. Discussions and projects are two examples. In other situations, don't require group work unless the focus is on a task that has a high degree of ambiguity or that requires far transfer. Here the benefits of negotiating a shared understanding will empower the desired outcomes.

The Surprise of Learning

In a new and interesting model, Karl Friston has proposed what is called the free energy principle. This principle states (in a very simplified view from the complex mathematics behind it) that we learn in order to minimize the difference between what we expect to happen and what actually occurs. We either adjust our models or change the way the world works. This makes sense in that we become better adapted to the world. There are nuances and implications.

First, the mismatch between our expectations and the outcomes is, in essence, a surprise. It also can be viewed as a failure, in that our predictions don't match what we expected to happen. Thus, surprise and failure are both useful tools in learning design. To support learning, it helps to make failure acceptable. Ideally, we want to avoid an environment where there are too-onerous expectations for success. Instead, we want an environment where failure is accepted, if not expected.

To predict what the world is going to do, we build and use causal models, as mentioned in chapter 3. And we will work to learn. We don't just sit in a dark room. We have drives (like hunger), but we're also driven to explore. My extension is that we'll explore if the consequences of the knowledge outweigh the consequences of getting it wrong. It's imperative that we make it safe to experiment!

Learning: Surprise is an important part of learning. We need to have our expectations challenged to be open to learning, and then models are valuable supports for improving our predictions. Failure has to be expected and made safe.

Activities

- Consider the contexts and types of practice to ensure that contextual changes don't undermine your learning designs.
- Revise your design process to put information into the world when you can, and into the head when you must.
- Create a way to explicitly consider when and how to use social learning appropriately, and follow it.
- Make exploration a natural and valuable part of the learning experience.

CHAPTER 5

Let's Get Emotional

- Noncognitive factors in learning
- Engaging experiences
- Learning culture

Has a smell or song or sound ever triggered a memory that you had completely forgotten? There's much more to memory than just the cognitive story. Humans are complex beings. Cognitive science, incorporating cognitive psychology but also neuroscience, sociology, anthropology, linguistics, and more, tries to be as inclusive as possible. Our approach will need to similarly be open-minded.

Cognitive science recognizes that there are drivers beyond our cognitive aspects. One model uses three labels to characterize the outcomes:

- **Cognitive:** the informal and formal reasoning we perform
- **Affective:** the feelings we have about things, likely influenced by our personality
- **Conative:** our *intention* to do things, dealing with motivations and any barriers

Depending on our mood and feelings at the time, our interpretations of a situation can differ. Similarly, if we're unmotivated or anxious about an experience, our ability to process it fully is impaired. This means that our intention to learn is one of the biggest determinants of learning success!

As we talked about in chapter 4, we're not the formally logical beings we once believed. The situated nature of our cognition means we can make snap decisions that we later explain with rational reasoning. What also plays a part in our decision making are these other, noncognitive aspects, which we typically lump under engagement.

What we're talking about is having an experience that's more than just presenting information and providing practice. People have to care, and want to change. And a number of things influence our learning in ways that go beyond a basis of cognitive thinking. This approach suggests, then, that considering what we know about emotion is a part of our learning science. We'll talk about personality, and then move on to topics like motivation and anxiety, which contribute to engagement.

We'll also talk about cultural elements that affect learning, such as making it safe to fail. The overall factors that influence learning include how you're introduced to it, your experience through the learning, and the environment in which it happens. The latter is worth exploring as well.

A Distinct Lack of Personality

Personality psychology (rejecting approaches based upon false premises, such as Myers-Briggs) has worked toward a suite of measurements that meet psychometric standards. Using a collaborative and open process, the field has converged on the Big Five elements, also known as OCEAN, for the five measures. The elements of openness, conscientiousness, extroversion, agreeableness, and neuroticism are used to characterize individual differences. It and a related model (HEXACO) are criticized for being atheoretical, generated out of factor analysis. Yet the results are robust (Figure 5-1).

These traits are characterized as relatively immutable, and it's not clear that designing for different personality styles makes sense. Instead, the robust results of research suggest that designing for the best learning outcome is the reliable approach. Consequently, the focus here will move to nonaffective elements. We do want to achieve feelings, but that's by design of the impact, not the personality affected. There may ultimately be important elements here, but not as of yet.

> **Learning:** Design for the learning, not the learner. That is, align the elements of models and examples to the practice that's appropriate to the desired outcome. Our learning objectives should be the determinant of the pedagogical approach. That does include understanding the learner audience, and any unique characteristics, but as of yet it's not a basis to adapt learning.

Figure 5-1. HEXACO Model

Factor	Traits of High Scorers	Traits of Low Scorers
Honesty; Humility (H)	sincere, honest, faithful, modest, unassuming, loyal	sly, deceitful, greedy, pretentious, hypocritical, boastful, pompous
Emotionality (E)	emotional, oversensitive, sentimental, fearful, anxious, vulnerable	brave, tough, stable, independent, self-assured
Extroversion (X)	outgoing, lively, cheerful, extroverted, sociable, talkative, active	shy, passive, withdrawn, introverted, quiet, reserved
Agreeableness (A)	patient, tolerant, peaceful, mild, lenient, gentle	ill-tempered, quarrelsome, stubborn, choleric
Conscientiousness (C)	organized, disciplined, diligent, careful, thorough, precise	sloppy, negligent, lazy, reckless, irresponsible, absentminded
Openness to Experience (O)	intellectual, creative, ironic, unconventional, innovative	shallow, unimaginative, conventional

Elementary, My Dear Engagement

There's robust evidence that things that evoke a strong emotional response are remembered better. To that point, in Nick Shackleton-Jones's book *How People Learn*, he posits that we remember only the emotional component. While that's an unlikely extension, it does make the point that we should make people care.

And, to be clear, engagement is a function of the elements we're talking about. Motivation, lack of anxiety, challenge, and more work together to create an experience that's compelling.

Engagement is complex. There's not even agreement about what are the core emotions. Yet, we know that there are positives and negatives. That is, some emotions are unpleasant (though sometimes we might indulge them), and some are pleasant (which we're more likely to seek).

At core, engagement involves more than the nervous system. Chemicals are emitted in tune with the triggers of our emotional state, and carry the messages. As a consequence, for instance, the long-term effects of negative emotions, such as stress, can actually damage the body.

Donald Norman, in his book *Emotional Design*, documented some elements of negative and positive emotions as well as the associated impacts on cognition. Not surprisingly, we are more open to explore, more divergent, and more relaxed when the emotional space was positive. Interestingly, we tend to dig deeper when the emotional environment was negative.

This isn't surprising, because under stress, we're likely to decrease our ability to marshal many cognitive resources, and will likely work hard in one area. At least initially, then, you want to keep the atmosphere positive. If our long-term goal is to be able to perform in stressful situations, that may end up being part of the experience design, but I'll suggest that getting the responses down before ramping up the pressure makes sense.

Anxiety

The negative reaction can be seen as a result of a core emotion, anxiety. Here I'm not talking about the general emotional state, but instead a specific dread of an anticipated learning experience. If we think things will go bad, it's certainly possible for anxiety to interfere with other events up to and including the dreaded one.

Learning certainly can spawn anxiety. If we believe the stakes are high, we might worry that we will not succeed. Our performance isn't as consistent as we'd like, and our architecture includes making mistakes occasionally. Stress can make that worse. Thus, if there's too much riding on one outcome, anxiety can interfere.

It turns out, according to research represented by the Yerkes-Dodson law, that a bit of arousal (read: stress or anxiety) increases performance (Figure 5-2). The question, of course, is how much is "a bit." Depending on your self-esteem, feeling of satisfactory practice, general even-headedness (such as low neuroticism on the OCEAN scale), and so on, you might go past the optimal level very quickly.

Our goal, then, should be to control anxiety and ensure that it's low enough to support learning. We'll address this more under culture, but in short we want the consequences of learning to not be too onerous compared with the benefits. So, for instance, we assign no weight to initial explorations, and model failure or tell stories of when *we* failed. Also, we want to allow people to develop at the rate they're comfortable. We don't necessarily need optimal performance, and the learning experience itself may be sufficient to support appropriate levels of anxiety.

Figure 5-2. Yerkes-Dodson Law

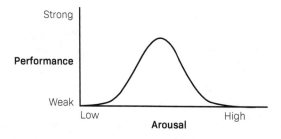

> **Learning:** We want to keep anxiety low (unless stress is a component of the learning experience, and then we want to introduce it appropriately). That means reducing the stakes of assessment, and developing competence and confidence to appropriate levels.

Motivation

A second core element is motivation. Do you learn best when you're unmotivated? The evidence suggests the answer is no. When we believe the experience will be irrelevant or boring, our intentions for the experience can be low. Some may stay away, some may mentally check out, and some have even paid their kids to click through content for them!

While massive open online courses (MOOCs) were experiencing completion rates around 10 percent (though with plausible explanations), e-learning was similarly experiencing a lack of commitment. Our desire to do better requires us to consider how to make experiences engaging.

Moreover, what makes experiences motivating face-to-face are hard to transfer online. Presence and active exercises can be challenging to replicate. It helps if we understand what's happening underneath, so we can *design* engagement, not just trust that it will emerge.

One of the most important distinctions is intrinsic versus extrinsic motivation. Intrinsic motivation comes from the learners' inherent interest in and awareness of the topic's relevance. Extrinsic motivation, basically, makes up for a lack of intrinsic interest with external motivators. The acronym PBL has been appropriated (from "problem-based learning") to represent "points, badges, and leaderboards."

A more sympathetic view of extrinsic motivation is an emphasis on drawing on game mechanics, proven through testing and a resulting experience of play. Scoring is one mechanism, as is an element of chance. Games can require role playing, decision making, and more. The question becomes what's designed in, and what's added later.

However, intrinsic motivation can come from role playing and decision making as well. When we place the learner in a role where the decisions they have to make reflect the ones they will need in the performance environment, we're tapping into inherent interest. If learners get that those decisions are relevant to them, they're more likely to be engaged. If the material isn't relevant, why are they learning it anyway? On the other hand, if it is, bring that relevance out, and make it clear!

Self-determination theory, as outlined by psychologists and professors Edward Deci and Richard Ryan, suggest that intrinsic motivation is rare. The model in Figure 5-3 was developed by Matthew Richter of the Thiagi Group and approved by Ryan as a simpler version of the full model.

Figure 5-3. Motivation Via Self-Determination Theory

Amotivation	Extrinsic Motivation			Intrinsic Motivation
	External	Internal		
Apathy	External Motivation *Incentives* *Points*	Introjection *Guilt* *"Should"*	Seeing Value *"Need"*	Passion *"Want"*

The model proposes various levels of extrinsic motivation, with internal extrinsic motivation being more typical. You can use gamification to get "external" intrinsic motivation, but more requires internal motivators. Guilt or a "should" response isn't as motivating as a recognition of "need" by seeing value. Of course, being motivated by wanting to know something is best, but harder to achieve through instruction.

Motivation starts *before* the experience really begins. We want to have learners eager for the experience. This can happen through advertising on a commercial basis, or when you have a captive audience, it can be the invitation. Regardless, you want to communicate the WIIFM (What's in it for me?), the intrinsic value.

Regardless of any invitation or prior announcement, you want to articulate the *why* at the beginning of the experience. We should introduce the audience to what they'll learn, touching on why they should care, and what it will provide for them. Opening up learners emotionally is an investment in the retention of learning.

Here our subject matter experts can help. They've spent years becoming expert in the topic. Why? What makes it so interesting? We can ask them! And we should. You may have to dig a tad deeper than "make the world a better place," but it's real. *And*, if whatever that characteristic is that makes it interesting doesn't work for the learner, maybe they're not cut out for this role.

To illustrate, a colleague found out that I knew games, and asked if I was willing to help him on a project. I said something like "Sure, what's it about?" He told me the topic was computer auditing. To my less-than-enthused response, he responded, "That's what I thought, too, but then I talked to them, and they said it was like playing detective. You track back to find the mistake. Most of the time it's just an error, but once in a while it's deliberate!" And that, right there, was the core of the game they were developing. Playing detective, and discovering the root of the problem! Finding what makes it interesting for the experts gives you a hook to help create interest in the learners.

Of course, we want to maintain motivation through the experience as well. We do that by not letting the experience drop below expected levels. We provide interesting examples, minimal models, and challenging practice. We also let learners know they're progressing.

John Keller, arguably the only instructional design theorist to consider emotions in learning, has developed and validated the ARCS model: attention, relevance, confidence, and satisfaction. That is, raise and maintain their attention, make the material relevant to them, build their confidence, and achieve satisfaction in the experience and the outcome. To me, the attention and relevance address motivation. We'll address confidence next.

> **Learning:** We want to build motivation before an experience begins. We will do it again at the beginning of the experience, and maintain it throughout. We want learners aware that this is of value to them. We can make it appealing aesthetically, but the real value is in the emotional pull.

Confidence

The other element that Keller's model supports, and is an otherwise underexplored topic, is confidence. While learners might not start with confidence in their ability, they can and should have confidence that the experience will develop their ability. And then we should build their confidence in what they are doing.

Ultimately, learners without confidence are less likely to perform when needed. If we haven't developed them to a level of confidence that they're willing to try when faced with the opportunity, we've failed. We need to go further. And while we can ask them, and there's no better way to assess emotional states, we also should be testing to see if we get application (which is, by the way, Level 3 of Kirkpatrick's training evaluation model), and refining until we do.

There's more to application than confidence, but personally I add it to retention and transfer as a third necessary outcome of learning. We build confidence in a couple of ways. For one, we support developing confidence by systematically developing skills at the appropriate level. We also want to be providing sufficient practice and feedback on progress until the learner both believes they can *and* has evidence saying the same. What exactly *sufficient* means may be a matter of testing and refinement.

In one sense, the confidence is the payoff of the initial motivation. We've delivered on the promise. We're also removing anxiety about performance. We want the emotional closure to be "I did need this, and now I've got it."

Learning: Build confidence in the learner by showing them their progress, and ensuring that they are improving.

Challenge

Building confidence comes from overcoming challenges. As you gradually master challenges you recognize are like the ones you'll see on the job, you can also recognize that your ability to handle them has increased. Thus, you can develop an expectation that you can achieve the goal.

Mihaly Csikszentmihalyi, the originator of the concept of flow, posited that a key element is the right level of challenge (Figure 5-4). When a challenge is within our capability, it's not of interest. When it's beyond our capability, we aren't eager to engage. In between is where we feel the experience of challenge. And, as we develop our abilities, it takes more to invoke challenge.

Figure 5-4. Flow

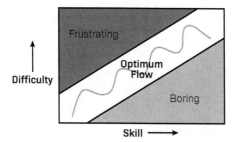

This aligns perfectly with Lev Vygotsky's zone of proximal development (ZoPD) we discussed earlier. We see that the emotional experience of challenge and the space for learning are the same. This is, by the way, the fundamental principle that, for me, explains why learning experiences are not only doable, but desirable. This means that learning will be optimized to the extent that we *make* it an experience! This is why game designer Raph Koster, in his *A Theory of Fun*, suggests that what makes games fun *is* learning.

> **Learning:** Manage the challenge level. Increase the challenge as the learner demonstrates competency. This ties in with confidence.

The Trajectory of Experience

Overall, I like to think of learning as an experience trajectory. This is my interpretation, not based in any empirical research. It's a synthesis of flow, anxiety, and motivation. It's also distilled from drama.

To start, recognize that dramas have a stereotypical trajectory of tension (Figure 5-5). It slowly builds, with mini-climaxes followed by releases. Still, dramas (and this includes comedies, adventure, and all other forms) will build to an ultimate climax, followed by the final outcome (the denouement).

This structure, simplified and exaggerated here, is seen across mediums—novels, theater, film—and represents a tested approach to engagement. If you've bought into the premise—the settings, characters, and goals—each new challenge leads to curiosity about how it will turn out, and fear for the protagonist.

Figure 5-5. Dramatic Tension

I think we should consider all the elements of subjective experience as we design learning. In addition to building capability, I think we should look to develop motivation, manage anxiety, and build confidence. A hypothetical trajectory could look like that in Figure 5-6.

Figure 5-6. Experience Trajectory

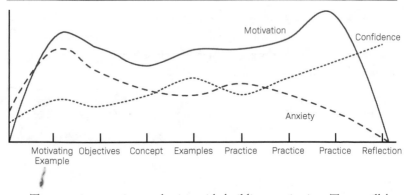

The experience trajectory begins with building motivation. There will be some anxiety, but we should make sure to keep it under control. And we'll want to gradually build confidence, and then maybe challenge that confidence, as we go. At the end, we no longer need motivation, because we have confidence. And anxiety should largely have disappeared.

Again, this is hypothetical, but is intended to be aspirational. We should be explicitly considering these elements and looking to design them in.

> **Learning:** Explicitly consider the emotions of the learner through the experience. Consider addressing motivation, anxiety, and confidence at the various stages of the learning process.

Just Joking

A difficult, but important, element is humor. The warnings are rife: Humor, done wrong, can be detrimental. And yet, when done well, humor assists—or so the research tells us. John Banas and colleagues summarized 40 years of educational research to point out how humor can be used positively or negatively, and how it can provide learning benefits.

The benefits of humor on memory are several. We've seen that positive affect, laughter, leads to more exploration. In addition, laughter gives a boost to memory retention. And, of course, it generates motivation and reduces anxiety. Good feelings also build a sense of community.

Humor targeted appropriately, or "on topic," facilitates learning. It may be best to incorporate humor before digging into the topic or wrapping up a section. That is, you might use jokes to prompt a segue from one topic to another or to close a section. Humor might also work to remove the stress of a challenging assignment, say by relaying your own or the expert's first attempt with the emotions and anxiety you or they encountered.

This brings us to the question, *how* do we do humor? The answer is more aesthetic than scientific, but there are some pointers. First, humor at another's expense is not appropriate. In general, mean-spirited humor doesn't work. Self-deprecating humor can, to an extent (which I find all too easy).

It's important to note that humor varies by culture. What is funny in Japan isn't quite the same as what's funny in Germany or the United States. This leads us to one possibility: Business and the workplace is the culture of, well, the workplace. So, recommendations to leverage the humor of the office make sense.

Scriptwriter John Vorhaus, in *The Comic Toolbox*, suggests that humor is "truth and pain," but we have to get there in an indirect way. The revelation is prompted by an unexpected twist. We have an expectation that things are going one way, and when the twist comes, it is explainable even though it's not expected. It's about a gap between the real world and the comic perspective.

The unexpected nature of humor can force people out of a work phase and indicate a break. Initial humor establishes a safe place, and regular (but not constant) humor can maintain that. It has to work both ways, of course; we have to tolerate appropriate humor among learners as well as by the teacher. So, we can crack a joke at the beginning (I begin my talks with a humorous incongruity, such as showing a really bad question), and break tension at particularly challenging moments with a pop culture reference appropriate to the audience. In general, humor should bookend meaningful interactions, but not interfere.

The humor should be relevant to the learning goals. Irrelevant humor can distract. Properly, humor should highlight having, or not, the knowledge being covered. Find natural ways in which the matter of the moment is the source of intrinsic humor. And don't have it be predictable; humor inherently is about unpredictability.

> **Learning:** Use humor appropriately. Use it lightly to establish a positive and shared learning environment, be culturally sensitive, and don't use it in the midst of a learning decision.

Getting Engaged

Ultimately, we want a framework that integrates these elements into a set of pre-scriptions for design. To that end, I surveyed a wide suite of approaches to engagement as part of my research on designing serious games. This included games, of course, but also theater, film, fiction, and product design. In short, I tried to explore everyone who'd written about experience. Further, my PhD student at the time, Rob Moser, continued that work and added in live-action role playing.

Ultimately, I synthesized that list into a suite of elements. Not every element appeared in every approach, but they all were repeated across approaches. This list was the basis for the engagement side of my first book, *Engaging Learning*:

+ Clear or emergent goals
+ Balanced challenge
+ Thematic coherence
+ Relevance: action to domain
+ Relevance: problem to learner
+ Choices of action
+ Direct manipulation
+ Coupling
+ Novelty

It's worth addressing each separately.

Clear or Emergent Goals

In games, you might start with one goal, and another may emerge. For instance, in a classic game, you awake in a bathroom with amnesia. Your initial goal is to figure out who you are and why you are there, but ultimately you're uncovering the evidence to convict the person who'd done it. You need goals, but they can shift.

Balanced Challenge

The right balance of skill and challenge achieves flow. As discussed earlier, too easy and it's boring; too hard and it's frustrating. Thus, you need to have a challenge that is at the appropriate level for the individual. And, that needs to adapt as the individual progresses.

Thematic Coherence

Here we're talking about the world in which the action is embedded. It might be set in the Wild West, medieval times, or outer space, but it needs to be consistent. Violations of world coherence interfere with engagement. Only a master such as Mel Brooks can break out of the setting, as he did in *Blazing Saddles*.

Relevance: Action to Domain

Here the action that is undertaken is fundamental to the goal. Being the score-keeper, for instance, isn't quite the same as being in the game. We want to have a goal, and a world, so that the action aligns.

Relevance: Problem to Learner

Here, we're saying that the world, the goal, and the necessary action to achieve the goal all are of interest to the learner. For instance, a sword-and-sorcery fantasy is likely to appeal only to certain populations.

Choice of Action

There should be different decisions to be made. (Or, as Brenda Laurel opined in her work on interfaces, at least the appearance of same.) Technically, a computer game is a series of multiple-choice questions (use this weapon, attack that opponent, run away, and so on).

Direct Manipulation

Bill Budge's game Pinball Construction Set was an inspiration for interface design. People didn't make good pinball games, but enjoyed the experience. It was the first "drag and drop" interaction available to the general public. The notion of building by placing flippers and bumpers and shaping boards illuminated the appeal of acting on a represented world. The ultimate realization was to minimize the distance between individual intentions and interface actions.

Coupling

The notion here is that there's a tight relationship between how you act on the world and how the world responds. In this sense, feedback comes from what happens as a consequence of your actions. Steve Draper called this "input-output inter-referentiality," an unwieldy but apt insight into the linkage.

Novelty

The unexpected is a hallmark of story. Even in *The Hero's Journey*, Joseph Campbell's distillation of the common elements across myths, there's a call to adventure that upends the protagonist's ordinary life. More broadly, it can be probabilistic outcomes in games (the proverbial roll of the dice), unexpected dialogue, or even side bits. A lack of predictability is a boon to creating experience.

Note that we'll revisit this list in chapter 8 (big reveal!).

> **Learning:** As an extension of the alignment of "flow" and the zone of proximal development, this set of synergistic elements goes beyond content and creating a learning experience. The take-home lesson is, of course, that learning can, and should, be "hard fun."

Cultured Learning

One other aspect comes into play here, and that's the culture of the learning environment. That is, what's the overall atmosphere that supports learning the best? Several elements contribute to optimal outcomes. Some of this comes from Amy Edmondson's work on informal and organizational learning with David Garvin and Francesca Gino, but transfers to formal learning as well.

Overall, they identified a suite of elements of culture, including leadership, concrete practices, and environment. It's the latter that is worth reflecting on here (Figure 5-7).

Figure 5-7. A Supportive Learning Environment

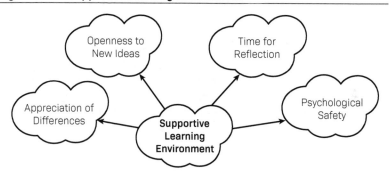

The first one is not just a tolerance, but an appreciation, of diversity. We know from studies on innovation that seeing things differently opens up new opportunities. Here, the different ways of viewing things, as we saw when we discussed social cognition, increases the likelihood that the emergent shared understanding is as rich as possible. This crosses any demographics that matter: ethnicity, gender, age, socioeconomic status. There does have to be a shared core: I'd suggest that a belief in the value of learning and working together are key.

A second one is an openness to new ideas. In organizational culture this means to avoid the "That's not how we do it here" syndrome, while for formal learning I suggest it's about being open to learning.

Time for reflection is remarkably missing in many (I'd say most) organizations, yet it is critical to allow incubation (percolation, fermentation—pick your metaphor) to occur. For formal learning, this suggests having time to allow learning processes to recover and also for new interpretations to emerge and be explored. In short, an event model is not conducive to learning not only for the spacing effect, but also for idea generation.

Finally, and arguably most important, is the notion of safety. Here it means that experimentation is not only expected but valued, and that it's okay to make mistakes. It's critical that learners can take their time and master the necessary components. Safety helps address anxiety, as mentioned previously. Techniques include removing evaluation (but retaining feedback) on many assignments, stipulating conditions of "evaluate behavior, not the person," and the instructor modeling making mistakes.

If, as said before, the learning context ultimately will be one of working under intense time or safety pressures, that can gradually be introduced, but the learning should still support mastering the component skills. And it shouldn't be personal; no one should be compared with others for the purposes of shaming.

> **Learning:** The environment in which learning happens matters. Factors in the environment can foster or hinder learning outcomes. Ensure that you've created the culture for learning as well as the practice and content.

Activities

+ Add a step in your design process to expressly create an initial motivational "hook" for the experience.
+ Extend engagement through the learning experience by ensuring that examples are captivating stories and practice is meaningful and appropriately challenging.
+ Create mechanisms to develop safety in your learning experiences, and use it.
+ Determine when and how you can use humor in your learning experiences, and adjust your design process accordingly.

CHAPTER 6

Going Meta

- Learning to learn
- Reflection
- General learning skills

In the days of the ancient Greeks, if not before, philosophers started thinking about, well, thinking. And yet it was several thousand years before we went beyond thought exercises to actual scientific study of our thinking. And now, we can think *about* our learning. This "meta-learning" or "learning to learn" can include instruction on effective learning, and self- and other evaluation of our learning. In fact, you shouldn't leave it to chance that your learners know the most effective ways to learn. Building in learning-to-learn is an opportunity to improve your learners beyond just the focus of a course.

There's general agreement that learning skills in particular domains are more powerful than skills that are cross-domain. So, for instance, learning how to make a business plan is going to be more useful to making business plans than just learning how to plan. However, there is also evidence that we can learn and apply more general learning skills, such as reading, or systematic experimentation. There are also attitudinal stances, like beliefs about who has responsibility for learning. And while there's much lip service about teaching meta-learning, the actual practice is irregular at best. We can do better.

This goal here is to fine-tune our learning. Being aware and consciously planning means we can be optimal in our approach. Monitoring means we can see how things are going. This is to both ensure that we're making progress and willing to change plans if necessary. And evaluating lets us know how we're doing, and allows us to experiment and try other things.

It's a mistake to assume we're good learners naturally. We *do* learn, but we're also prone to certain beliefs about learning that aren't efficient. And while schools and organizations should not leave these to chance, the sad thing is that they do. However, we do not have to.

Being active *about* the learning process, not just *in* the learning process, is a big opportunity. You can affect an individual's success as well as the organization's. The notion of a learning organization is that there's not only an environment that's conducive for learning, but explicit practices to do so. Those practices include documenting and promoting what good learning is and not taking it for granted, but actively developing these skills.

There are specific learning skills, such as self-explanation. We can also cultivate mindsets such as open-mindedness and conscientiousness. Emphasizing that intelligence and ability aren't fixed, and that persistence is valuable, can help develop a useful approach to learning.

Different learning and processing skills must be distributed across learning. They can't be a singular focus, but instead must be seeded across a more consistent learning process. However, they need to be practiced in the context of another topic. You need something to be learning *about*.

Tracking them is a separate effort, which systems are generally not designed to accommodate. This is an area for technology development, but it shouldn't be ignored. These skills can and should be developed, not assumed. This means that we can and should layer actions about how to use information on top of the actual learning. We can start small, then gradually make it more sophisticated.

> **Learning:** Don't leave meta-learning to chance. Build in specific references to skills. Consider actually assessing and developing them as part of your overall curriculum.

Thinking About Thinking

Meta-learning started with meta-cognition, the concept that we can think about our own thinking. The notion is we can look at our mechanisms for gathering information and processing it.

Harold Jarche's Personal Knowledge Mastery, with its "seek-sense-share" framework, is a nice way to look at it (Figure 6-1). In my interpretation of his framework, seeking is about both active searching and setting up a system that feeds interesting new tidbits. Ideally there'd be a bit of serendipity in there. Sensing is about processing the information. I see two major ways here: re-representing the information (which can include synthesizing it in the context of other information), and experimenting by trying out what is understood. Sharing, of course, is making clear what the outcomes are for others to learn from. It's about showing your work, as Jane Bozarth has advocated for, whether to all or submitted to specific others. This brings the opportunity to get feedback and start the process again.

Figure 6-1. Seek-Sense-Share

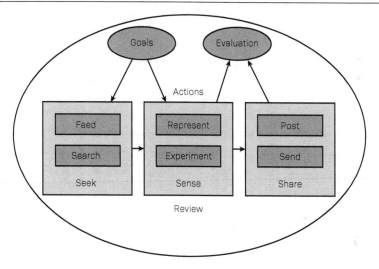

The goal here is to not only set this up, but systematically review the outcomes. Properly done, it's an instance of "double loop" learning, where you apply your seek-sense-share to your seek-sense-share. Yes, it's all very recursive and, well, meta!

Improving on the history of meta-cognition, our modern interpretations, as evidenced in the chapters on emergent phenomena, show where our understanding has gone. But it's also about the tools we can use to support us.

One of the artifacts of our cognitive architecture is gaps in our memory. Our long-term memory reconstructs concepts, not exact details. This means we're really bad at rote memory, more so for large quantities or arbitrary knowledge. With our limited working memory, we're also bad at complex calculations. We've developed mechanisms to cope, including checklists, decision trees, and reference books.

It turns out, digital technology is the opposite of us. Our devices are bad at pattern-matching and meaning-making (for now), but they can remember rote and arbitrary information perfectly, and calculate as complexly as we can program them to. We can use our tools to make us smarter.

This starts with being explicit *about* our thinking: our plans, progress, and outcomes. We can offload this, and even do some tracking. This applies to thinking, but also to learning. In practice, meta-cognition is largely *about* learning, because most of what we want to think about is new things.

Learning About Learning

The distinction between learning and innovation blurs here. When we're doing design, research, and problem-solving, we don't know the answer when we start. Thus, inherently, we're learning. And most of our cognition is *about* such topics. So it's *about* learning!

Yet formal learning is different. It's not someone doing it on their own; instead, it's a scaffolded process. As a consequence, we have the opportunity to support learners *acquiring* learning to learn skills. Thus, we should be explicit about what we can do and how.

For instance, there are results about approaches to learning. Note taking, despite being almost ubiquitous, turns out not to be that effective. Nor does rereading, or highlighting. Ways to usefully process the material (instead of just recording it) include rephrasing what's said, drawing pictures, or mind-mapping (Figure 6-2).

Figure 6-2. A Mind Map of Mind-Mapping

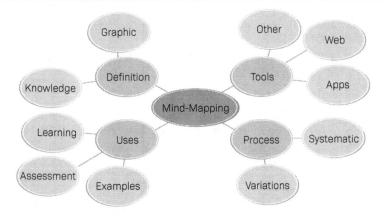

In their book, *Evidence-Informed Learning Design*, Mirjam Neelen and Paul Kirschner made the distinction between self-directed and self-regulated learning. Their distinction is at the level of operation. The former is about learners choosing their performance needs and associated learning goals. The latter is about addressing a specific learning goal by making a plan and evaluating progress.

In a sense, self-directed learning isn't about formal learning at all. It takes the steps of the seek-sense-share model and applies it to one's particular situation. It's about addressing one's specific interests and needs, not what a curriculum tells you.

Self-direction in learning has to do with learners deciding whether they want to continue to specialize in this, or add in some aspects of that. Facilitating that is a job for a counselor. What we can influence is self-regulated learning.

Self-Regulated Learning

While meta-cognition in general is thinking about thinking, when we apply that to accomplishing tasks, we talk about meta-cognitive regulation. Meta-cognitive regulation consists of three steps:

- **Planning:** being conscious of your own thinking or learning, and matching approach and priority to the need
- **Monitoring:** checking that the plan is being followed and adapting as needed
- **Evaluating:** reflecting and looking at the outcomes and determining if the same approach or a new one should be used in the future

Self-regulated learning is applying these steps to your own learning goals.

Your intent should be to develop the ability of your learners to *be* effective, self-regulated learners. That is, you would like them to take ownership of the material. As learners move from novices to practitioners to experts, their needs change (Figure 6-3). Novices move from not knowing what they need or why it's important to knowing what they need and why when they become more practiced practitioners. Then, once they hit expert level, no one has to tell them what they need, and instead experts reflect and have creative interactions with other experts to advance their knowledge.

Other elements that accompany the transition include the increasing value of informal learning methods. Coaching and mentoring cross the boundary from formal to informal. Personal and collective learning (such as collaboration on tasks and on community improvement) further the transition from practitioner to expert.

Figure 6-3. The Transition From Formal to Informal With Expertise

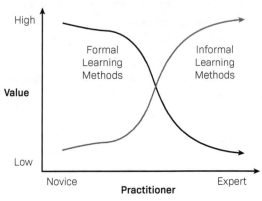

Adapted from Ted Cocheu.

It's not necessary that it happens, but I suggest it's desirable. I also argue that the responsibility shifts to the community of practice, but I think that designers for formal learning can and should facilitate this. There are practical steps that can be taken.

Most important, our choices of actions for them can gradually be handed over. We should increasingly ask learners to start choosing content to access and deliverables as well as format and annotation. Thus we add in opportunities for learner choice.

An accompanying responsibility is to make our learning design philosophy clear. It would be hard for learners to reverse-engineer our approach, and being explicit about choices is valuable. In personal experience, it's removed complaints such as "Why this practice task?"

As learners start taking on responsibility for the learning tasks, they're internalizing the pedagogy and becoming self-improving learners. If they're required to justify their choices as part of the reflective rationale, you have a basis for instructors to not only address their domain learning, but also their personal learning approach.

Having learners evaluate the efficacy of their approaches is also desirable and possible. That is, they should track their predictions and outcomes, and be encouraged to consider alternatives. This is also an area where social interaction comes into play.

Leaving evaluation to chance isn't a good choice. Learners' assessments of the value of a learning experience have been shown to have a low correlation with the real impact. Similarly, their learning preferences have likewise demonstrated little correlation with what actually works for them. Thus, being explicit about learning practices is important.

This is not something that you do on its own. Learning to learn skills *have* to be developed when learning something else. To do this successfully requires two specific adaptations. First, you have to track the learning-to-learn skills separately from the topic. Thus, most extant systems don't handle this well. A second requirement is that the variability and spacing in practice for a topic also applies to the learning-to-learn skills. So, you could be tracking and developing a systematic approach to experimentation, or self-explanation skills, and you'd likely need to practice those *across* topics (or they could become context-bound).

This may seem like a lot of extra work, but I'll maintain that it becomes a small matter of habit and doesn't intrude. Instructors should have both pedagogical and domain knowledge, and addressing both is important. If necessary, you can have teams sharing the responsibilities, but ultimately building these skills is an investment not just in your learners, but also in your organization's ability to learn.

> **Learning:** Don't assume effective learning skills on the part of your learners. Be explicit about what makes effective learning, and consider actively evaluating and developing these skills.

Attitudes Toward Learning

Attitudinal elements are frequently considered part of domain skills, but there's some evidence that your beliefs about learning affect your learning as well. Despite some controversy, there are some reasons to believe that it matters.

One of the more compelling proposals was for the benefit of persistence. As defined by Angela Duckworth, grit was touted as a specific indicator of success. That is, persistence was an independent contributor to success separate from intelligence. This certainly makes a plausible story.

The story has been confounded, however, by personality science. As previously mentioned, the best indicator of personality characteristics has been the collaborative and open psychometric endeavor termed variously as the Big Five or HEXACO. The conscientiousness dimension, in particular, has been touted to be correlated with grit or persistence. Thus, it's not clear whether this is truly an independent concept. Regardless, the trait is valuable, and it may be amenable to intervention as a habit or practice.

An alternative formulation has more potential power. Carol Dweck introduced the distinction between a "fixed" and a "growth" mindset, which distinguishes between whether you believe your intelligence is predetermined or your knowledge and success can be influenced by hard and appropriate work. While controversy reigns here as well, it's also a plausible hypothesis.

Both are instances of how your beliefs about learning (in philosophy, this is known as epistemology: what you believe about the nature of knowing) can influence your success. If you believe that your efforts are unimportant to the outcome, you may unconsciously undermine them. One recommendation is to reward sincere effort, rather than facile accomplishment.

While the ability to alter these beliefs is uncertain, currently there's no reason to suggest the contrary. For the very least, people *can* learn new things. Good learning design makes a difference, too.

> **Learning:** While you may not be able to change beliefs about learning, demonstrate a commitment that persistence and effort do make a difference.

Reflecting on Reflection

Another useful process in learning is reflection. This often accompanies feedback, in that the learner takes time to review their performance. More extended reflection makes sense in contexts of more complex performances.

Reflection can be personal or it can be facilitated. Facilitating reflection can include asking learners to actively synthesize and communicate their resulting understanding. They can write, diagram, or other activities.

Learners can also be asked to revise work outputs produced by practice. Here they're practicing again with refinements to their process, demonstrating an improved understanding.

Reflection can be individual or in a group as well. Learners can reflect on their own work, or on group work. Similarly, groups can reflect together on individual efforts, or on a group effort, collaboratively creating a new output.

In a sense, we're developing the learner's ability to self-evaluate, and consequently to internalize that and self-improve. It's meta-learning in that you also have the chance to ask learners to reflect on their own learning: Not just how they did, but how they could learn better next time. Acquiring a habit of reflection can be a valuable step in learning to learn.

> **Learning:** Consider creating opportunities for learners to reflect on their learning, individually or collectively. When possible, create concrete evidence of their actions and progress. Also, make opportunities for them to express their own understanding.

Future Thinking

So-called 21st-century skills have come under attack, with respect to their definitions and our ability to develop or evaluate them. So here I want to address a specific subset of skills that, like meta-learning skills, cross domains but are important to develop explicitly—at least until we can count on K–12 or higher education to develop them.

First, some folks argue about the specific definitions. When people complain about job definitions that ask for creativity or flexibility, I agree. These are hard to empirically measure, and thus to evaluate. Some of that (specifically, creativity) is subject to many external factors, such as culture and process. Others, however, are tangible, I suggest.

There are a variety of lists of these skills, such as those created by blue-ribbon panels, universities, or individuals. They feature a wide variety of proposed inclusions—five, seven, 12, 13 . . . the list goes on. Without anointing any particular suite of skills, it's important to be aware of them and choose the set that makes the most sense to you. The point is to figure out which ones can be evaluated and developed. Having a competency-based definition would be a necessary requirement.

To me, what counts are skills that cross domains and topics—basic success skills. And we should be able to define a performance as a competency, à la Robert Mager. That is, we can specify:

- **Performance:** what it is
- **Context:** when it's relevant
- **Criteria:** how we determine if it's done correctly

If we can do so, we can develop it. Categories of skills include things like the ability to communicate: putting together a cogent story whether via presentation or document. Another candidate would be the ability to build a model, whether numeric or symbolic. Working well with others can be tracked as well. The point is not to dictate the specific skills, but look to the same mechanisms—varying and tracking across domains—that characterized meta-learning skills. Again, requiring extra effort, but ultimately adding a unique value proposition: developing the learner as well as the learning.

The way this manifests in learning is to have activities that combine both applying domain knowledge and 21st-century skills. So, for instance, analyze numbers to make a business plan, and then create a presentation to present the analysis. There can be support and evaluation of the analysis and the presentation, as well as the business plan. Make the skills explicit, and develop them over time along with the domain knowledge.

> **Learning:** Don't assume effective generic skills on the part of your learners. As with meta-learning skills, be explicit about what makes effective learning, and consider actively evaluating and developing these skills.

Activities

+ Consider explaining your pedagogical design, in brief, in your learning experiences.
+ Be clear about what you are assuming as learning skills on behalf of your learners, and determine when you should make help or recommendations available.
+ Build time and activities for reflection in your experiences.

CHAPTER 7

Implications

- The elements of learning experience design
- Getting serious about learning

From a learning perspective, what's experienced tends to revolve around a suite of elements that form certain cognitive and emotional functions. And when we design, we (should) develop in a different order than the learner experiences them. While I've tried to highlight the take-home lessons, here I want to view them from the perspective of design and learner experience. The intersection of those two is a critical component of succeeding at learning experience design.

I'll take us through the steps that traditional instruction prescribes for the experience, not the order in which you should design the experience. I cheat with the first one, because the learning objectives we design to shouldn't be seen by the learner (as is), but they're critical to get the rest right.

For the record, the order you should design in is:

- **(Objectives):** so you know what your learning goals are
- **Practice(s):** you should first design your final assessment to test your ultimate objective, and then prior ones to prepare the learner and provide for retention
- **Concept(s):** here you design the model that will guide performance and provide a basis for feedback
- **Example(s):** the stories that show how the concepts are applied in context (or not), and the breadth to ensure appropriate transfer
- **Introduction:** the emotional and cognitive hooks
- **Closing:** the emotional and cognitive closure

The main thing for design is to specify the practice immediately after the objectives, and save the bookend sections for the end.

Through the Eyes of the Learner

For now, we're going to go through the steps in the order of learner experience: (objectives), introduction, concept, example(s), practice(s), and closing. Note that there may be iterations from practice back to concepts or examples before more practice.

(Objectives)

The objectives are the guide to designing the learning. Ideally, they're in the form of competencies (emphasizing *do*, not *know*). You need to consider the barriers to obtaining the objectives. That compilation approach to memory, where expertise is inaccessible to conscious knowledge, means you can't just take what experts say; you need to dig deeper.

Let's be clear, these are *not* the objectives you show to learners. These are the ones you design to, and they should be clearly about performance. If you show objectives to the learner, they should be rewritten (another learning from science) to be ones that learners will care about. That's not the same criteria we use to design.

Then, you should represent objectives in ways that you can measure. Robert Mager's format works well here:

- **Performance:** what they have to be able to do
- **Context:** when and where they have to do it
- **Criteria:** how you determine that they've done it

Specific recommendations include:

- Don't take what the subject matter experts (SMEs) provide as a given. Work to unpack what learners need to be able to do.
- Ensure that you represent accurately the performance context(s), and how you can tell it's been performed to a sufficient level.

Introduction

The introduction is what hooks the learner and prepares them for the learning experience. There are both emotional and cognitive elements (with overlap). Emotionally, you want learners to understand why this is relevant for them, building motivation. Cognitively, you want to activate relevant knowledge, making the learning process more effective.

One element is to start with a motivating example, illustrating *why* this is relevant to the learners. The goal is to hook them emotionally before addressing the cognitive aspects. Note that a motivating example is not the same as a traditional example. The goal here is not to portray the actual process of applying concept to context, but instead making an emotional hook. The example can humorously or dramatically portray the negative consequences of not having the knowledge, or the positive consequences of having the knowledge.

There should also be a clear exposition of the "What's in it for me?" (WIIFM). And, to be clear, that is *not* the objectives we use for design! Instead, learner-focused objectives are what they will get out of the experience *that they care about*. This may be evinced from the motivating example, but can also be separately introduced.

Expectations can also be set about the experience that is to come. This is particularly important if it will violate their expectations about what's coming.

To set the right atmosphere, the experience can make it clear that the expectation is that they can make mistakes. Even if ultimately there will be pressure, it's important to let learners know (and manifest concretely in the experience) that the goal is for them to succeed.

Finally, it's worthwhile to drill down from the broader context into why they're getting *this* learning, now. Emotionally we've addressed why they should care, but cognitively we should make it clear why this learning is important as well.

Specific recommendations include:

+ Make it meaningful.
+ Make it safe.
+ Proactively address any dissonance between expectations and experience.

Concept(s)

The concept is the underlying model that allows learners to predict the outcomes of their actions in this situation. This is the basis they use to decide what to do. Typically, it's a causal set of relationships that explain what has happened or will occur. The diagrams I've used to this point are what I'm talking about (Figure 7-1).

Figure 7-1. Models

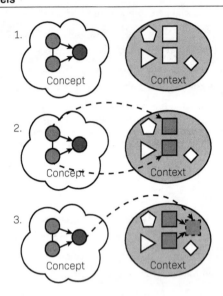

In this example, the model is mapped to the context, and then the model provides a basis for making an inference. We're using a model to explain models, but what we're talking about is making conceptual and causal relationships that support appropriate inferences.

Models are also used as guides for performance. Many times, they're ways of thinking that help shape your performance. In sports, for instance, we have metaphors about how to address a number of flaws ("Look the ball in"). Ultimately, we tend to internalize the relationships (and they may no longer match our initial explicit understanding).

Multiple models help. My personal explanation for this is that more ways of thinking about a situation increase the matching points people may find to models. This means more patterns are activated to match to the current situation. And finally, whatever one does get triggered can trigger others, and there are more ways to look at a problem to work toward a solution.

Specific recommendations include:

+ Use diagrams or animations, mapping conceptual relationships to spatial ones.

- If possible, use multiple models to help increase the likelihood of access and finding a solution path.
- You get these models from experts, but not without work; a process helps.

Example(s)

Examples show the concept being applied in a particular context. They should communicate the current situation, the goal to be achieved or problem to be solved, the steps, *and the underlying thinking*.

A good example has a narrative story that helps learners better imagine the problem and the goal (Figure 7-2). It explicitly references the model that guides performance, using it to show how the concept maps to the context. And it shows the underlying thinking—not only the result, but the rationale about *why* it was done that way.

Figure 7-2. Example Elements

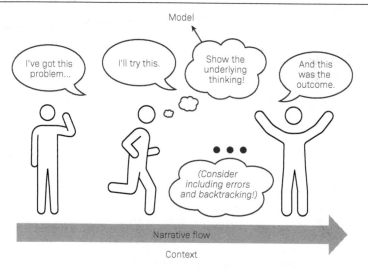

As mentioned earlier, the spread of contexts matters. The contexts that span practices and examples determine the scope of transfer. That is, you can abstract and apply to the space of contexts you've seen, but you're less likely to transfer outside that space.

Work by Alan Schoenfeld, as unpacked in Allan Collins, John Seely Brown, and Ann Holum's seminal paper, "Cognitive Apprenticeship," shows the value of including backtracking and repair. Here, the expert models working toward a solution, recognizing a problem, and stopping. The expert backtracks, finds the error, and moves forward. All, of course, while verbalizing the associated thinking. While experts don't like showing mistakes, this process is valuable for learners to see and internalize self-monitoring.

Different media can be used. Narrative text, a labeled or narrated series of images, a graphic-novel or comic format, or documentary-style video all can work. Variety can provide desirable novelty, as long as there's not too much cognitive load.

Specific recommendations include:
- Ensure a sufficient spread of contexts that captures a representative sample of the full space of applicability.
- Tell a story; make it interesting.
- Show the underlying thinking and tie it to the model.

Practice(s)

Practice is the core of learning. With practice *and feedback*, you can shape your behavior, though biologically, secondary learning goals likely will need explicit models and examples. You want people to be able to make good predictions so as to make good decisions. The elements that make practice work should be included in the task, the contextualization, and the feedback.

First, practice has to be the *right* next task. That is, it's got to be the right thing for the learner at this time. Looking at the zone of proximal development, it's not too simple to be easy, but also not too difficult to be impossible. It should focus on the next thing the learner needs. And that is, of course, also the appropriate level of challenge.

We've also established that practice needs to be spaced and varied. That is, you need to have a chance to sleep and try again another day, and another, and another. This indicts, by the way, most workshop models of a concentrated day or several. The latter can work if you reactivate, and both can work if you follow up at appropriate times, but in general a concentrated workshop can't significantly develop skills without appropriate support. Also, mixing it up matters. This all supports retention of the learning over time.

The right contexts, in conjunction with the examples, help support transfer. The spread of contexts chosen determine areas of high likelihood for transfer. The choice of practice contexts, coupled with example contexts, should represent the desired scope of application.

The context for practice can be directly related to the task at hand, or it can be fantastic (in the sense of invoking an unreal situation in any number of familiar dramatic situations). For specific tasks and near transfer to known contexts, using those contexts is likely to be appropriate. It has been suggested that if far transfer is needed, or the material needs some learning-context excitement to map to the normal job-performance excitement in real situations, setting the task in a fantasy setting may be appropriate. This is not yet, to my knowledge, empirically demonstrated. The essential element is not to lose the core task in adapting to the fantasy.

Feedback is a critical component of effective practice. Ideally, it's specific to *this* performance of the learner. It should explicitly reference the model, and explain why the response was, or wasn't, appropriate on that basis.

The alternatives to the appropriate choices should not be random, silly, or easy. Generating the appropriate level of challenge means having misconceptions that represent ways learners go wrong at this level of difficulty. Having the learners make addressable mistakes in the learning experience is preferable to making those mistakes in real performance.

Specific recommendations include:

+ Choose a meaningful context for the task.
+ Ensure the right task for this learner (at this time).
+ Space out practices.
+ Vary practice tasks and difficulty.
+ Provide meaningful feedback.

Closing

Ultimately, we will finish the learning experience. It's about releasing the learner cognitively, and closing the experience emotionally. This involves several components, some typical and some less frequently seen.

For starters, the effort of the learner should be recognized. They've expended effort, and it should be acknowledged.

This can be coupled with announcing the learner's accomplishment. They've achieved new capabilities, and this should be signified. They can even be introduced into the appropriate community of practice.

This should be paired with a recontextualization. Just as we drilled down from the broader context into the rationale for this particular learning, we should drill back up, connecting their accomplishment to the bigger picture of the world.

Two types of further direction are worth pointing out. For one, the learners might be interested in going into more depth, and pointers to more material on the topic are relevant. For another, learners are now ready for new things. These new directions should also be pointed out.

Specific recommendations include:

+ Close the emotional experience.
+ Close the cognitive interest.
+ Point out further directions.

Getting Serious

Not all learning misses the elements of learning science. Typically, we see certain elements missed. What differentiates the elements we're talking about from what we see too often? It's worthwhile to see the implications through different iterations, so this is another take.

In 2013, four of us learning science aficionados were attending yet *another* e-learning exposition. And, we realized that while there were shiny new objects and attention-gleaning buzzwords, nothing fundamentally had changed. We were still seeing the same old e-learning.

We cared, so we wondered what we could do. And thus was born the *Serious eLearning Manifesto* (elearningmanifesto.org). While it's called the *eLearning Manifesto*, we very much believe the e is silent. It's just that our areas of recognition are largely based in e-learning, and we didn't want to be too presumptuous. However, we believe that all of the items, except perhaps the last, are true for all learning, not just digitally mediated experiences.

My co-conspirators included Julie Dirksen, author of the well-regarded *Design for How People Learn*; Will Thalheimer, one of our most preeminent translators of research to practice; and Michael Allen, of Authorware fame and an e-learning leader over decades. We ultimately proposed eight values that we thought separated typical e-learning from serious e-learning (Figure 7-3).

Figure 7-3. The Serious eLearning Manifesto

Typical E-Learning	Serious E-Learning
Content focused	Performance focused
Efficient for authors	Meaningful to learners
Attendance driven	Engagement driven
Knowledge delivery	Authentic contexts
Fact testing	Realistic decisions
Didactic feedback	Real-world consequences
One-time events	Spaced practice
One size fits all	Individualized challenges

We backed these eight values with 22 principles based upon decades of research around the globe. And made it freely available for use with only attribution. We encourage you to sign on! (No one expects you to get it all done in one go.) The eight values explained:

+ Focus on **performance first**. If you're not trying to help people *do* things differently, why are you bothering? This is really a call to do some performance consulting first, so that you verify a learning experience is the needed solution.

+ Also, learning needs to be **meaningful to learners** in both ways identified previously: anchored as a real application, and relevant to learners. It isn't about efficiency; it's about effectiveness.

+ And the experience should be **motivating**; learners should get why they should engage. This is about the emotional component, making it motivating and addressing anxiety.

+ Learning, as discussed previously, happens best in **real contexts**. Again, they can be fantastic, but the knowledge application in the environment has to be appropriate.

+ The decisions learners see in the learning experience should reflect those in the **performance environment**. We're trying to avoid "inert" knowledge.

- The **consequences** of those decisions should be made manifest. Learners should know what happens as a choice, to build appropriate models.
- Practice has to be **spaced**. Our brains need time to rest between activating and strengthening, and we want to ensure sufficient strengthening.
- Ideally, there is **individualized challenge**. This can come from the different practices you create. While it's possible to do this without technology, it doesn't scale well. With technology, you *can* sequence problems depending on how people do individually.

This is another filter through which to view effective learning experiences, and you will notice overlap with the elements of effective practice previously developed. That's to be expected and desired.

Activities

- Ensure that your learning is focused on meeting real needs and what learners should *do*, not *know*.
- Create a checklist that looks at the important criteria for each element (intro, models, examples, practice, closing) and use it to ensure that the important criteria are being met.

CHAPTER 8

Putting It All Together

- What this looks like in practice
- A new curricula
- Moving forward

Ultimately, we need to pull all these elements together into experiences that educate and engage. Here, we're looking at how the elements form a coherent outcome. We'll explore a sample using an integrative framework, then consider implications for curricula as well, before looking forward.

Social anthropologist Jean Lave observed Brazilian street children as part of her research. She found that they were capable of sophisticated financial transactions. Yet these kids couldn't do the typical math at school. The disconnect led her to propose that learning should reflect enculturation into a community of practice rather than the traditional instructional approach. She called her approach "situated learning." This emphasizes the nature of situated cognition mentioned earlier.

Subsequent frameworks echo this understanding. As mentioned before, Allan Collins and John Seely Brown framed Cognitive Apprenticeship as an instructional model that focused on "situated" cognition. They synthesized the approaches of three areas of research—Allen Schoenfeld in mathematics, Ann Brown and Annemarie Sullivan Palincsar in reading, and Marlene Scardamalia and Carl Beiter in writing—into a generic approach to cognitive skills. I suggest cognitive skills are what will define the necessary abilities in the information age.

In short, I suggest that organizations won't be changed by the ability to recite facts, but instead by the ability to make better decisions. Decision making is the cognitive skill at the core of performing, problem solving, and more—decisions about what to do, when, and how. And this informs what we teach as much as how we teach. It's not about reciting facts; it's about the ability to *do*.

Cutting to the Quick

I maintain that learning is action and reflection. At least, the important learning that will differentiate us as individuals and support organizational success. I don't believe that rote recitation, for instance, will achieve either one.

If learning is indeed action and reflection, this implies that proper instruction is designed action and guided reflection. That is, we should be carefully designing learning experiences that elaborate important elements and support appropriate retrieval practice. There must be feedback, and time for reflection on that feedback. The performance objectives should be focused on how learners apply the knowledge to solve problems, on meaningful action. And then the learners should see how they're doing.

Our goals for learning are retention over time and transfer to all appropriate (and no inappropriate) situations. Whatever we train, be it marketing, sales, finance, logistics, product or service development or delivery, or customer support, we need people to be able to perform in the workplace. Retention, as we discussed, requires spacing to strengthen long-term memory. Transfer requires both sufficient breadth of examples and scaffolding of reflection to support appropriate abstraction. This reflection can consist of both models and examples, whether presented or developed by the learner through experience and guidance.

On top of that, we want to hook the heart as well as the mind. We want to successfully meld the emotional with the scientific. How do we integrate the rigor of effective education with the experience of engagement?

At the Intersection of Learning and Engagement

Many years ago, in the course of identifying components of effective learning games, I synthesized a list of elements of effective education practice. This list came from many different learning and instruction theories, such as cognitive theories of learning, instructional design approaches, social learning theories, and more. I admit I've even looked at machine learning to try to see what might be inferred. And they're very much focused on *doing*. Not every element was seen in every theory, but each emerged again and again. The elements were:

+ Clear goals
+ Appropriate challenge
+ Contextualized

- Anchored
- Relevant
- Exploratory
- Active manipulation
- Appropriate feedback
- Attention getting

I think it's worth going through each one separately. The work came from reflections on having developed a game for learning. But first, an important point to note here is the absolute congruence of these elements and those from chapter 5 about the elements of engaging experience (Figure 8-1)! (Back to "hard fun.")

Figure 8-1. Alignment Between Education and Engagement

Education	Engagement
Clear goals	Clear or emergent goals
Appropriate challenge	Balanced challenge
Contextualized	Thematic coherence
Anchored	Relevance: Action to domain
Relevant	Relevance: Problem to learner
Exploratory	Choices of action
Active manipulation	Direct manipulation
Appropriate feedback	Coupling
Attention getting	Novel information and events

This is the fundamental awareness that sparked *Engaging Learning*, my book on learning-game design, and suggests that we can methodically integrate engagement with effective education. (Systematic creativity is *not* an oxymoron!) To make it more practical, particularly for those unequipped with the resources for full games, I'll use another example.

Under the auspices of Learnnovators, a bespoke e-learning provider, I had written a series of posts on deeper e-learning. Looking to practice what we preach, with the company's sponsorship and partnership, we created a project to demonstrate the principles under real-world constraints. This demo, Workplace of the Future, was done as a tribute to our late friend and author of *Informal Learning*, Jay Cross. We recruited my colleagues in the Internet Time Alliance (ITA), which Jay had formed, to address learning in the modern workplace.

This demo had four modules (one from each remaining ITA member). The focus was on workplace practices that reflect alignment with what's known about how people work best. Module topics were information flow, meaningful work, working "out loud," and communicating safely. For each, there were several activities, and a streamlined information resource.

Through the Workplace of the Future example, we'll examine the elements of effective education practice in more detail.

Clear Goals

The activity to be undertaken, the practice, should have a clear definition of what the outcome should be. Whether it's a product or an outcome of a scenario, learners need to know what they're trying to achieve. It should be specifically tied to the competence definition derived from the performance objectives.

In the case of Workplace, the goals were stipulated in each activity in the model. For example, in one, your goal was to convince the CEO to support developing the social network (Figure 8-2). In another activity, it was to provide feedback to an employee in a productive way.

Figure 8-2. Goals

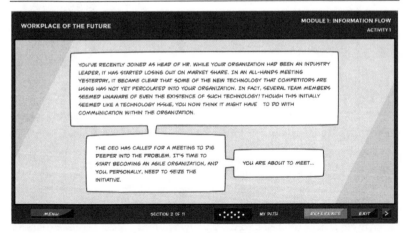

Appropriate Challenge

Lev Vygotsky's zone of proximal development model suggests that there's a level of challenge necessary for learning. If it's too easy, it's accomplished without thought. If it's too challenging, learners can't succeed and no learning can occur. If it's in the zone in between, where they can succeed with support, learning occurs. This means that questions with silly or obvious wrong answers don't accomplish any meaningful outcome.

In Workplace, the alternatives to the right answer were designed to be subtle and represent mistaken ways people often act (Figure 8-3). With specific feedback for each choice, there wasn't one generic response to all choices. There also was an explicit avoidance of obvious or silly responses.

Figure 8-3. Challenge

Contextualized

As pointed out, learning works better in concrete situations. Abstract problems don't get activated in real situations. Facilitating abstraction (or guiding reflection) from concrete problems helps develop transferable skills. Choosing the right set of contexts to support appropriate transfer becomes an important component.

The activities in Workplace were in workplace settings with characters that reflected various roles. The learner would be given appropriate goals to achieve that reflected the particular office. We used a cartoon look to deliberately support contextualization that could still be interpreted by learners into a familiar context.

Anchored

John Bransford and the Cognition and Technology Group at Vanderbilt talked about anchored cognition, or having the decisions embedded in the learning process. That is, learners can comprehend the goals in context as being real uses of the knowledge. If they're not plausibly appropriate, they won't accept them. Note that the design doesn't have to be realistic (games can be set in space, the Wild West, or elsewhere), but it has to naturally incorporate the necessary decisions.

In Workplace, the decisions were chosen to support better problem solving and teamwork under pragmatic constraints. The pushbacks could be on costs, or individual goals. These reflect real office concerns.

Relevant

For learning design to be relevant to the learner, the learner actually has to care about the problem being addressed. The goal has to be something that is meaningful *to them*. This is a twist on "anchored"; for learning to be anchored, the design must be a real application of the knowledge, and to be relevant, the learner has to care about the application of the knowledge.

The Workplace activities were chosen to reflect the difficult choices that organizations face and that L&D has the opportunity to address. The initial setting that kicked off each activity made clear the problem that needed to be addressed.

Exploratory

Good design doesn't just give the learner given the answer. It allows them the ability to try out different alternatives. That is, there are different options to select from, with different outcomes.

In Workplace, there were always different choices with different outcomes to explore (Figure 8-4). We used branching scenarios in most of the activities, reflecting the natural dance of conversation that dialogue entails.

Active Manipulation

Exploration has to have consequences. Learners have to not just see the options and outcomes but choose among them and live with (and learn from) the outcomes.

In Workplace, scenarios had outcomes that were not ideal (Figure 8-5). You could fail to achieve the objectives, and have to try again. There were consequences to choices, and suboptimal outcomes provided feedback but suggested revisiting the decision to gain the necessary understanding.

Figure 8-4. Exploration

Figure 8-5. Active Manipulation

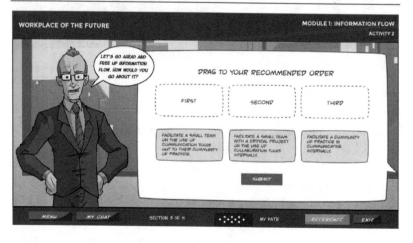

Appropriate Feedback

Learners need feedback to understand the relationship between their choices and the model of the world they need to understand. We want learners to build causal models of the world that lead to the right predictions. That comes from the relationship between their choices and the feedback. And, of course, the right feedback addressing their particular misconceptions.

For Workplace, those consequences *were* feedback. However, additional feedback was provided that linked the choices back to the underlying models (Figure 8-6). There were models for each module, but they were not presented up front, and instead were available on demand. They were also minimal, by design.

Figure 8-6. Feedback

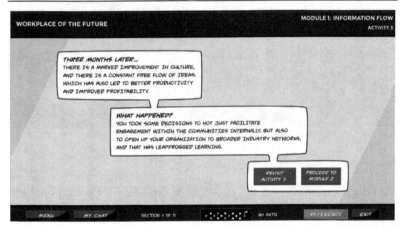

Attention Getting

You need to maintain attention through the learning experience. It helps to capture it initially, but you should also be aware of maintaining it throughout the learning experience.

Activities in Workplace, as branching scenarios, couldn't use probability. Instead, we put idiosyncrasies in the characters, and the organizational products. We also had odd bits of dialogue in various parts of the branches, so that there were unexpected bits of humor (Figure 8-7).

The important point is to recognize that these elements are critical to creating learning experiences that are effective *and* engaging.

Figure 8-7. Unexpected

Learning: Serious games are, perhaps, the ultimate learning experience. Putting people into the role of making contextualized decisions is an ideal practice for learning. We can approximate that fairly closely without having to build, or develop to, a full game engine.

Curriculum Anew

Another issue is going beyond the pedagogy to the curriculum. The perspective on action, on doing, that we started with suggests a new curriculum as well as a refined pedagogy. Curriculum, sadly, has been characterized by a content focus. That is, the decisions about what to learn have been dictated by knowledge statements. This, I suggest, is wrong. I'll propose an alternative (Figure 8-8).

Figure 8-8. A Different Basis for Curricula

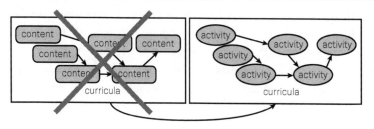

The principle of designed action and guided reflection implies that curriculum should be based on activities (Figure 8-9). If we're developing meaningful performance objectives, then they're doing things that have outcomes. So what's assigned is not topics to be learned, but projects to be accomplished. This is a project-based, problem-based, or goal-based approach, as others have termed it. The emphasis is on *do*, not *know*. The activities drive, naturally, a need for the content. The output of those activities is some sort of product, whether a trace of action in a simulation or a concrete output such as a plan, design, model, or communication. And each is annotated by reflection, the thinking behind the choices. Together, the product and reflection create a portfolio of work.

Figure 8-9. An Activity-Based Curriculum

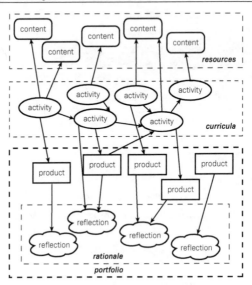

The products and associated reflections generated by the activities provide a basis for evaluation, and all choices are an opportunity for mentoring. The products naturally invoke tools and require so-called 21st-century skills, such as design and communication. This model extends in several ways. The activities can build upon one another, for one. They can be done individually or in groups, for another (Figure 8-10).

Figure 8-10. A New Curriculum Model

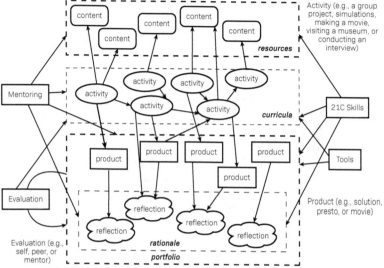

An extension to this, the self-directed learning extension to self-regulated learning, is that gradually, learners are given the chance to choose the activities, content, products, and mode of reflection. This develops their ability to become self-improving learners. As discussed in chapter 6, an important entailment, then, is that the learning design philosophy must be made visible. The choices learning designers make about the series of activities need to be available. Thus, learners can internalize the pedagogical principles to develop their ability to make their own choices (Figure 8-11).

This view of curriculum, as a series of activities, complements and reflects learning experience at the macro level as well as the micro level of individual activity design. And yes, this was an editorial soapbox, but an important one. Standing down.

Learning: Just as our pedagogy should focus on doing, not on knowing, so too should our curriculum. We should be building meaningful tasks from component tasks. These naturally embed concepts, whereas the reverse isn't the case.

Figure 8-11. A Meta-Learning Pedagogy

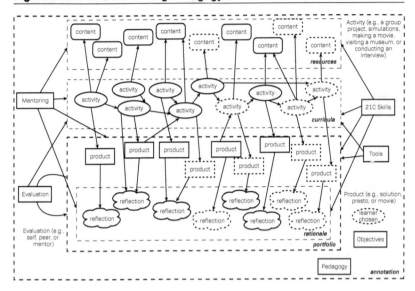

Ever Onward

As we near the end of this book, let's be clear about one point. There's much more to learning science than what's here. There are conferences, journals, and more all dedicated to this field of endeavor. And ongoing research. There's no way you can be expected to stay on top of it. Yet, your professional obligation is to try. What can you do?

Be a Consumer

First, read. ATD has a science of learning content area; the Learning Guild has a research library, as well as its *Learning Solutions* magazine; the Learning Development Accelerator has a learning science focus; and *eLearn Magazine* regularly publishes work at the intersection of research and practice. There are also many useful books (see the bibliography, for instance). There are tweeters and bloggers as well who either convey, or point to, valuable information. You *can*, of course, read journals in the original academese. This is recommended but not expected.

Second, listen. There are podcasts and recorded speeches, perfect for commutes or excursions. Audio versions likely exist for some of the more popular books.

Third, engage. Go to conferences, attend workshops, sign up for webinars, and take courses. And don't passively consume what's presented. Ask yourself: "What does this mean I should do differently?" If you can't imagine the consequences, ask. If you don't understand what the instructors say, or if you want to dig deeper, ask.

And, of course, stay engaged. Track the "translators." There are some main contributors, but new folks pop up over time (and others retire).

Also track related fields. Much of what has made it into our design approaches comes from fields that have innovated practices that make sense for us to co-opt. We co-opted agile design approaches from software engineering and participatory design from user experience.

Harold Jarche's Personal Knowledge Mastery approach, again, is a useful practice. His framework consists of three elements: seek-sense-share. In his formation, you should create a set of inputs that brings new information to you (in addition to searching for specific needs). And review it. You should also be processing what comes in, actively. That includes representing your take and experimenting. And you should share your outcomes with others. We all benefit.

Be Critical

Be smart, of course. There's a lot of hype out there, and you need to not accept what anyone tells you uncritically. You need to determine who's trustworthy, and then have your own process to address new proposals.

The translators have established a reputation for integrity and insight about research proposals. They don't always have to agree, but even their disagreements are insightful.

You also need a process to follow. Daniel Willingham has a systematic, four-step process, whereas Carl Sagan had nine steps. My take is similar to Willingham's, with four steps:

+ Sniff it.
+ Strip it.
+ Track it.
+ Evaluate it.

The first step is to see if it passes the sniff test. This basically is a quick reality check for plausibility. Do your instincts suggest this is valuable, or does something seem "off"? While intuition isn't always right (see learning styles), particularly if it's not in an area of personal expertise, it can be a good guide. The main thing is to see if there's a credible causal story. If not, you can stop there.

If it passes the sniff test, the next step is to strip it down to the bare bones: What, specifically, should you do differently, *and* what would you expect as an outcome? One thing this does is remove irrelevant things from consideration. And it helps to know what you'd do, and what it'd cost, versus the purported benefits. Willingham also includes a "flip it" step in his "strip it" step, which looks at the alternative. That would be one way to check for credibility; is the alternative story legitimate?

If it seems plausible and relevant, then it's time to see where this is coming from. Track it back—who's saying this, on what basis; what vested interest to do they have; and, arguably most important: Who *else* is saying this? Don't just rely on anecdotes from happy customers; they have an interest in believing it's worthwhile, because they've already invested. Instead, look for independent data from someone who doesn't benefit if you buy it. Are there multiple credible sources pointing to this as a valid approach? And who's arguing against it? Resist "our proprietary research says . . ." Sad to say, sales and marketing are not always above making spurious claims.

If it passes these tests, you might want to look at the work they're citing as a credible case. If it's published in a peer-reviewed journal of some credibility, you may be done. However, the real test is to look into the details. For instance, did they use subjects that are like the folks you're working with, did they use appropriate methods and analysis techniques, and did they carefully qualify how far these results can be extrapolated?

Really, you're just applying learning science to technology evaluation. And that's the smart thing to do. It's the way you check on whether you're being a responsible steward of your organization's resources.

Invest Smartly

Ultimately, be mindful of the admonition "Caveat emptor" ("Buyer beware"). You should wait to invest until you know the real benefits you should get, and they should outweigh the cost. You want to employ a return-on-investment analysis that justifies the cost.

I'll make one more admonition: Get the basics right *first*. It's easy to get excited about new technologies: VR, AI, adaptivity, microlearning. (Remember when we thought video or virtual worlds were the end-all, be-all?) Applying learning science correctly and then adding in new technologies is going to be a much better investment than just going for the new technologies. I've been known to say, "If you get the design right, there are lots of ways to implement it; if you don't get the design right, it doesn't matter how you implement it."

I'll suggest that the *best* investment you can make is focusing on learning science. If you have meaningful practice, even if it's not adaptive, it's better than having adaptivity on a content dump. Similarly, having the right model in 2D is likely to be more valuable than no model in VR. Gilded bad design is still, after all, bad design.

Conclusion

Applied learning science is a necessary step to successful instruction. It's likely the best investment you can make. It requires work to comprehend, and to stay current. But really, is that any different from any other profession?

Medicine, law, music, engineering—everything evolves. So too does our understanding of our own brains. We really have, for instance, no real explanation for consciousness. Yet, we have lots of really valuable guidance for designing learning outcomes that will persist. We just need to apply it.

I hope you feel better prepared to design instruction, face claims for new approaches, and create experiences that achieve the outcomes we need. So now, go forth and do so!

Activities

+ Commit to making learning experiences that are effective and engaging, not just events.
+ Ensure that your curricula, not just your courses, are focused on doing, not just knowing.
+ Establish support for yourself, and if relevant, your team, to continue to learn and grow.
+ When in doubt, experiment.

Collected Learnings

Chapter 2

Ensure that any information you want learners to perceive is detectable. Using appropriate channels for information and providing sufficient duration is important. For instance, give learners control over dynamic media so they can pause or restart it; otherwise, information could be lost.

Consider accessibility. There are potential limitations in your audience. First, design so that there are redundancies, such as augmenting color with pattern. Second, provide alternatives, such as text of any audio. Third, provide support for alternative mechanisms, such as screen readers.

We need to help learners focus. Remove distractions that can add to cognitive load. If the ability to perform with noise or stress is part of the context, get the processing down first, then add in the extraneous factors. Second, help learners direct their attention appropriately. Integrate labels into diagrams, and use pointers or spread out messages to introduce things one by one.

Don't overload working memory. Keep the amount of information being processed at a low level. This includes contextual and conceptual knowledge. We can overload the system easily.

Help learners chunk necessary information. Given that we can hold only so many bits of information, support the general building of those bits. Be very clear about what has to be in the head, and what can be in the world. And then determine explicitly what should be considered as a whole concept. We want to ensure that what's represented in short-term memory is useful based on the context.

We need to support encoding and retrieval. Have learners elaborate the information to explain things in their past that are related to the performance need. And provide retrieval practice in the same mode as they'll need to use it. For instance, elaborate coaching by thinking of previously observed or experienced coaching situations, and have them retrieve your coaching information to use to accomplish a coaching goal. Provide connections for learners, or support them in generating relationships between the knowledge to be learned and their preexisting knowledge.

Knowledge structures are fluid. Provide sufficient practice to ensure that an appropriate level of discrimination between concepts is present when needed.

Match the instruction to the learning. The learning outcome should dictate what's an appropriate form of practice, and the necessitated knowledge in support.

Make the assessment tasks mimic the real-world tasks. Even if it's via multiple choice, have the question mimic the decision one needs to make, not the knowledge one needs to make it. If that knowledge needs to be automated, do so, but then have learners apply that knowledge. Otherwise, question why it's needed.

Chapter 3

Feedback should be impersonal, clear, minimal, and delivered upon completion of the practice. It should not only provide the outcome, but also explain why the answer was wrong and what would be correct.

Present models of causal relationships that provide a basis for predictions and explanations. Use them in examples and in feedback on practice.

Use the misconceptions people have in your learning design. Make your alternatives to the right answer common ways that people get it wrong. And address each mistaken approach individually.

Choose an appropriate suite of concrete contexts, spread across examples and practice, to support the needed transfer, near or far.

Ensure that the task requirements, with all the elements, are within the learner's reach (if not their grasp). Test to ensure that the requirements don't exceed learner capability.

Support appropriate automatization. This is like the previous recommendation to support chunking, but here it's about taking those designed chunks and ensuring sufficient practice and feedback to support taking the use of the chunks from conscious to rote.

Retrieve in the way to be used. If people need to *use* information to make decisions, have them do that, not merely demonstrate that they know the information.

Space learning out over time. Massed practice in an event model isn't likely to lead to sufficient retention. Build spaced practice into your learning model, and into your design process.

If you can, mix up the practice and manage challenge level. Switch from this element to that, which helps make it less predictable. Try to make the challenge level appropriate for where the learner is.

Take a second pass at your writing to trim it!

In general, use the right media for the message. You can mix it up to maintain variety for novelty's sake, but don't undermine the essential message. And consider comic or graphic-novel formats.

Chapter 4

The situated nature of our cognition means we can be prone to insufficiently transferring knowledge from one context to another. So, in addition to sufficient practice to support retention, we also need to consider the contexts of practice. We want to ensure that our practice contexts span the space of applicability—that is, cover all the situations we want the learner to apply the knowledge in. The practice contexts don't have to cover every situation, but instead cover sufficient breadth so that we'll appropriately transfer to those situations we didn't see in practice.

Don't put in your head what can be in the world. Our brains are very bad at remembering large quantities of information, particularly if it's arbitrary, and similarly bad at complex calculations. Digital technology is the reverse. We should determine what can be in the world first, and then design learning to accommodate those resources.

Use social learning activities when appropriate. That includes showing modeled examples (including the instructor modeling the behavior), and using group work when conditions are right.

Social learning is both powerful and costly. We need to be clear about when and how to use it. In situations like formal education, where learners are expected to regularly convene, use that time for important collaborative work. Discussions and projects are two examples. In other situations, don't require group work unless the focus is on a task that has a high degree of ambiguity or that requires far transfer. Here the benefits of negotiating a shared understanding will empower the desired outcomes.

Surprise is an important part of learning. We need to have our expectations challenged to be open to learning, and then models are valuable supports for improving our predictions. Failure has to be expected and made safe.

Chapter 5

Design for the learning, not the learner. That is, align the elements of models and examples to the practice that's appropriate to the desired outcome. Our learning objectives should be the determinant of the pedagogical approach. That does include understanding the learner audience, and any unique characteristics, but as of yet it's not a basis to adapt learning.

We want to keep anxiety low (unless stress is a component of the learning experience, and then we want to introduce it appropriately). That means reducing the stakes of assessment, and developing competence and confidence to appropriate levels.

We want to build motivation before an experience begins. We will do it again at the beginning of the experience, and maintain it throughout. We want learners aware that this is of value to them. We can make it appealing aesthetically, but the real value is in the emotional pull.

Build confidence in the learner by showing them their progress, and ensuring that they are improving.

Manage the challenge level. Increase the challenge as the learner demonstrates competency. This ties in with confidence.

Explicitly consider the emotions of the learner through the experience. Consider addressing motivation, anxiety, and confidence at the various stages of the learning process.

Use humor appropriately. Use it lightly to establish a positive and shared learning environment, be culturally sensitive, and don't use it in the midst of a learning decision.

As an extension of the alignment of "flow" and the zone of proximal development, this set of synergistic elements goes beyond content and creating a learning experience. The take-home lesson is, of course, that learning can, and should, be "hard fun."

The environment in which learning happens matters. Factors in the environment can foster or hinder learning outcomes. Ensure that you've created the culture for learning as well as the practice and content.

Chapter 6

Don't leave meta-learning to chance. Build in specific references to skills. Consider actually assessing and developing them as part of your overall curriculum.

Don't assume effective learning skills on the part of your learners. Be explicit about what makes effective learning, and consider actively evaluating and developing these skills.

While you may not be able to change beliefs about learning, demonstrate a commitment that persistence and effort do make a difference.

Consider creating opportunities for learners to reflect on their learning, individually or collectively. When possible, create concrete evidence of their actions and progress. Also, make opportunities for them to express their own understanding.

Don't assume effective generic skills on the part of your learners. As with meta-learning skills, be explicit about what makes effective learning, and consider actively evaluating and developing these skills.

Chapter 8

Serious games are, perhaps, the ultimate learning experience. Putting people into the role of making contextualized decisions is an ideal practice for learning. We can approximate that fairly closely without having to build, or develop to, a full game engine.

Just as our pedagogy should focus on doing, not on knowing, so too should our curriculum. We should be building meaningful tasks from component tasks. These naturally embed concepts, whereas the reverse isn't the case.

References

Bozarth, J. 2014. *Show Your Work: The Payoffs and How-To's of Working Out Loud*. San Francisco: Pfeiffer.

Clark, A. 1996. *Being There: Putting Brain, Body, and World Together Again*. Cambridge, MA: MIT Press.

Clark, R.C. 2020. *Evidence-Based Training Methods*, 3rd ed. Alexandria, VA: ATD Press.

Cross, J. 2007. *Informal Learning: Rediscovering the Natural Pathways That Inspire Innovation and Performance*. San Francisco: Pfeiffer.

Csikszentmihalyi, M. 1990. *Flow: The Psychology of Optimal Experience*. New York: Harper & Row.

Dirksen, J. 2015. *Design for How People Learn*, 2nd ed. New Riders Press: Berkeley, CA: New Riders Press.

Duckworth, A. 2016. *Grit: The Power of Passion and Perseverance*. New York: Scribner.

Dweck, C. S. 2006. *Mindset: The New Psychology of Success*. New York: Random House.

Ericsson, A., and R. Pool. 2016. *Peak: Secrets From the New Science of Expertise*. Boston: Houghton Mifflin Harcourt.

Gawande, A. 2010. *The Checklist Manifesto: How to Get Things Right*. New York: Metropolitan Books.

Hutchins, E. 1996. *Cognition in the Wild*. Boston: MIT Press.

Kahneman, D. 2011. *Thinking, Fast and Slow*. New York: Farrar, Straus and Giroux.

Keller, J.M. 2010. *Motivational Design for Learning and Performance: The ARCS Model Approach*. New York: Springer.

Koster, R. 2006. *A Theory of Fun for Game Design*. Scottsdale, AZ: Paraglyph Press.

Kuhn, T.S. 1962. *The Structure of Scientific Revolutions*. Chicago: University of Chicago Press.

Lave, J. 1988. *Cognition in Practice: Mind, Mathematics and Culture in Everyday Life*. Cambridge, UK: Cambridge University Press.

Mager, R. 1975. *Preparing Instructional Objectives*, 2nd ed. Belmont, CA: Lake Publishing.

Malamed, C. 2015. *Visual Design Solutions: Principles and Creative Inspiration for Learning Professionals*. San Francisco: Wiley

McClelland, J.L., D.E. Rumelhart, and PDP Research Group. 1986. *Psychological and Biological Models*. Vol. 2 of *Parallel Distributed Processing: Explorations in the Microstructure of Cognition*. Cambridge, MA: MIT Press.

Neelen, M., and P.K. Kirschner 2020. *Evidence-Informed Learning Design*. London: Kogan-Page.

Norman, D.A. 1990. *The Design of Everyday Things*. New York: Doubleday.

Norman, D.A. 1993. *Things that Make Us Smart*. Reading, MA: Addison-Wesley.

Norman, D.A. 2003. *Emotional Design: Why We Love (Or Hate) Everyday Things*. New York: Basic Books.

Quinn, C.N. 2005. *Engaging Learning: Designing e-Learning Simulation Games*. San Francisco: Pfeiffer.

Quinn, C.N. 2011. *Designing mLearning: Tapping Into the Mobile Revolution for Organizational Performance*. San Francisco: Pfeiffer.

Quinn, C. 2018. *Millennials, Goldfish & Other Training Misconceptions: Debunking Learning Myths and Superstitions*. Alexandria, VA: ATD Press.

Rumelhart, D.E., J.L. McClelland, and PDP Research Group. 1986. *Foundations*. Vol. 1 of *Parallel Distributed Processing: Explorations in the Microstructure of Cognition*. Cambridge, MA: MIT Press.

Ryan, R.M., and E.L. Deci. 2017. *Self-Determination Theory: Basic Psychological Needs in Motivation, Development, and Wellness*. New York: Guilford Publishing.

Sagan, C. 1997. *The Demon-Haunted World: Science as a Candle in the Dark*. New York: Ballantine Books.

Shackleton-Jones, N. 2019. *How People Learn: Designing Education and Training That Works to Improve Performance*. London: Kogan Page.

Shank, P. 2017. *Write and Organize for Deeper Learning: 28 Evidence-Based and Easy-to-Apply Tactics That Will Make Your Instruction Better for Learning*. Self-Published.

Vorhaus, J. 1994. *The Comic Toolbox: How to Be Funny Even If You're Not.* Beverly Hills, CA: Silman-James.

Vygotsky, L.S. 1978. *Mind in Society.* Edited by M. Cole, V. John-Steiner, S. Scribner, and E. Souberman. Cambridge, MA: Harvard University Press.

Wiggens, G., and J. McTighe. 1998. *Understanding by Design.* Alexandria, VA: Association of Supervision and Curriculum Development.

Willingham, D.T. 2012. *When Can You Trust the Experts? How to Tell Good Science From Bad in Education.* San Francisco: Jossey-Bass.

Recommended Resources

Allen, M., J. Dirksen, W. Thalheimer, and C. Quinn. n.d. "Serious eLearning Manifesto." elearningmanifesto.org.

Ambrose, S.A., M.W. Bridges, M. DiPietro, M.C. Lovett, and M.K. Norman. 2010. *How Learning Works: Seven Research-Based Principles for Smart Teaching.* San Francisco: Jossey-Bass.

Bandura, A. 1963. *Social Learning and Personality Development.* New York: Holt, Rinehart, and Winston.

Brandon, R.N., and N. Hornstein. 1986. "From Icons to Symbols: Some Speculations on the Origins of Language." *Biology and Philosophy* 1: 169–189.

Bransford, J.D., A.L. Brown, and R.R. Cocking. 2000. *How People Learn: Brain, Mind, Experience, and School.* Washington, DC: National Academies Press.

Brown, P.C., H.L. Roediger III, and M.A. McDaniel. 2014. *Make It Stick: The Science of Successful Learning.* Boston: Harvard University Press.

Carey, B. 2014. *How We Learn: The Surprising Truth About When, Where, and Why It Happens.* New York: Random House.

Clark, R.E., and F. Estes. 1996. "Cognitive Task Analysis." *International Journal of Educational Research* 25(5): 403–417.

Cognition and Technology Group at Vanderbilt. 1990. "Anchored Instruction and Its Relationship to Situated Cognition." *Educational Researcher* 19(6): 2–10.

Collins, A., J.S. Brown, and A. Holum. 1991. "Cognitive Apprenticeship: Making Thinking Visible." *American Educator* 6(11): 38–46.

Duckworth, A.L., C. Peterson, M.D. Matthews, and D.R. Kelly. 2007. "Grit: Perseverance and Passion for Long-Term Goals." *Journal of Personality and Social Psychology* 92(6): 1087–1101.

Friston, K. 2010. "The Free-Energy Principle: A Unified Brain Theory?" *Nature Reviews Neuroscience* 11(2): 127–138.

Garvin, D.A., A.C. Edmondson, and F. Gino. 2008. "Is Yours a Learning Organization?" *Harvard Business Review*, March. hbr.org/2008/03/is-yours-a-learning-organization.

Jarche, H. 2013. "Personal Knowledge Management." jarche.com/wp-content/uploads/2013/03/PKM-2013.pdf.

Keiras, D.E., and S. Bovair. 1983. *The Role of a Mental Model in Learning to Operate a Device*. Office of Naval Research Technical Report No. 13.

Kruger, J., and D. Dunning. 1999. "Unskilled and Unaware of It: How Difficulties in Recognizing One's Own Incompetence Lead to Inflated Self-Assessments." *Journal of Personality and Social Psychology* 77(6): 1121–1134.

Learnnovators. n.d. "Workplace of the Future." learnnovators.com/workplace-of-the-future/story.html.

Merrill, M.D. 1983. "Component Display Theory." In *Instructional Design Theories and Models*, edited by C. Reigeluth. Hillsdale, NJ: Erlbaum Associates.

Merrill, M.D. 2002. "A Pebble-in-the-Pond Model for Instructional Design." *Performance Improvement* 41(7): 39–44.

Merrill, M., D.L. Zhongmin, and M.K. Jones. 1991. "Instructional Transaction Theory: An Introduction." *Educational Technology* 31(6): 7–12.

Miller, G.A. 1956. "The Magical Number Seven, Plus or Minus Two: Some Limits on Our Capacity for Processing Information." *Psychological Review* 63(2): 81–97.

Minsky, M. 1985. *The Society of Mind*. New York: Simon & Schuster.

Nielsen, J. 1997. "How Users Read on the Web." Nielsen Norman Group, September 30. nngroup.com/articles/how-users-read-on-the-web.

Rumelhart, D.E., and A. Ortony. 1976. "The Representation of Knowledge in Memory." Chapter 4 in *Schooling and the Acquisition of Knowledge*, edited by R.C. Anderson, R.J. Spiro, and W.E. Montague. Hillsdale, NJ: Lawrence Erlbaum Associates.

Schank, R., and C. Cleary. 1995. *Engines for Education*. Hillsdale, NJ: Erlbaum Associates.

Shute, V. 2007. *Focus on Formative Feedback*. RR-07-11. Research Report, Educational Testing Service.

Spiro, R.J., P.J. Feltovich, M.J. Jacobson, and R.L. Coulson. 1992. "Cognitive Flexibility, Constructivism and Hypertext: Random Access Instruction for Advanced Knowledge Acquisition in Ill-Structured Domains." In *Constructivism and the Technology of Instruction*, edited by T. Duffy and D. Jonassen. Hillsdale, NJ: Erlbaum Associates.

Sweller, J. 1988. "Cognitive Load During Problem Solving: Effects on Learning." *Cognitive Science* 12(2): 257–285.

Thalheimer, W. 2006. "Spacing Learning Events Over Time: What the Research Says." Work-Learning Research.

Thorn, K. 2018. "The Value of Instructional Comics for eLearning." Learning Solutions, August 3. learningsolutionsmag.com/articles/the-value-of -instructional-comics-for-elearning.

Index

Page numbers followed by *f* refer to figures.

About the Author

Clark Quinn assists Fortune 500, education, government, and not-for-profit organizations in integrating learning science and engagement into their design processes. He has a track record of innovation, and has consistently led development of advanced uses of technology, including mobile, performance support, and intelligently adaptive learning systems, as well as award-winning online content, educational computer games, and websites. Previously, Clark headed research and development efforts for Knowledge Universe Interactive Studio, and held management positions at Open Net and Access CMC, two Australian initiatives in internet-based multimedia and education.

Clark is a recognized scholar in the field of learning technology, having held positions at the University of New South Wales, the University of Pittsburgh's Learning Research and Development Center, and San Diego State University's Center for Research in Mathematics and Science Education. He earned a PhD in cognitive psychology from the University of California, San Diego, after working for DesignWare, an early educational-software company.

Clark keynotes both nationally and internationally and is the author of numerous articles and chapters, as well as the books *Engaging Learning: Designing e-Learning Simulation Games*, *Designing mLearning: Tapping Into the Mobile Revolution for Organizational Performance*, *The Mobile Academy: mLearning for Higher Education*, *Revolutionize Learning & Development: Performance & Innovation Strategy for the Information Age*, and *Millennials, Goldfish & Other Training Misconceptions: Debunking Learning Myths and Superstitions*. In 2012 he was awarded the eLearning Guild's first Guild Master designation. He blogs at Learnlets.com, tweets as @quinnovator, and serves as executive director of Quinnovation.